PRIMARY CURRICULUM DESIGN & DELIVERY

PRIMARY CURRICULUM DESIGN & DELIVERY

GLYNIS FRATER

CORWIN

SAGE Publications Ltd
1 Oliver's Yard
55 City Road
London EC1Y 1SP

CORWIN
A SAGE company
2455 Teller Road
Thousand Oaks, California 91320
(800) 233-9936
www.corwin.com

SAGE Publications India Pvt Ltd
Unit No 323-333, Third Floor, F-Block
International Trade Tower, Nehru Place
New Delhi – 110 019

SAGE Publications Asia-Pacific Pte Ltd
3 Church Street
#10-04 Samsung Hub
Singapore 049483

Editor: James Clark
Assistant Editor: Diana Alves
Production Editor: Neelu Sahu
Copyeditor: Peter Williams
Proofreader: Bryan Campbell
Indexer: KnowledgeWorks Global Ltd
Marketing Manager: Dilhara Attygalle
Cover Design: Naomi Robinson
Typeset by KnowledgeWorks Global Ltd
Printed in the UK

Library of Congress Control Number: 2022951115

British Library Cataloguing in Publication data

A catalogue record for this book is available from the British Library

ISBN 978-1-5297-8993-5
ISBN 978-1-5297-8992-8 (pbk)

At SAGE we take sustainability seriously. Most of our products are printed in the UK using responsibly sourced papers and boards. When we print overseas we ensure sustainable papers are used as measured by the PREPS grading system. We undertake an annual audit to monitor our sustainability.

CONTENTS

ABOUT THE AUTHOR

Following several years teaching in schools in the West Midlands and Shropshire, Glynis's professional journey then led her through several different incarnations of policy change in relation to curriculum design and delivery. She was a part of the introduction of the Key Skills Support Programme and led on building a strategy in Wales for the embedding of key skills into the curriculum in Key Stage 2 and 3. She was a Programme Director working with the Specialist Schools and Academies Trust developing a Continuing Professional Development (CPD) strategy for schools across England and Wales as part of a rethinking of the curriculum before 2010. In 2010 she founded Learning Cultures Limited, an organisation dedicated to developing high-quality CPD for school and subject leaders, teachers and others in education. She has been an integral part of the design and delivery of high-profile curriculum and coaching programmes and training courses for primary and secondary audiences across the UK and internationally. She is also a qualified coach. Coaching is an essential element of creating a high-quality and deeply collaborative CPD strategy in any organisation and Glynis continues to weave the principles of coaching into all her work. She is the author of and contributor to several Business Studies textbooks, has written for educational journals and creates a weekly news-post for the education profession through Learning Cultures' website. Glynis lives in Shropshire with her husband and Toby the dog.

ACKNOWLEDGEMENTS

Writing a book is a time-consuming and all-encompassing endeavour. It is a personal and solitary journey for the writer which can leave colleagues, friends and family slightly out of the writer's orbit. I would like to say thank you to all those who have patiently supported me in writing this book and who have encouraged me along the way. Alison Buck and Sarah Mackay have made sure that the business side of Learning Cultures continues with great skill and care. Lee Taylor and Sandra Stansfield, two exceptional coaches, have kept me up to date with anything I have missed in relation to education policy and the world of coaching and CPD. I have taken inspiration, knowledge and a deeper understanding of curriculum matters from many of the headteachers and their teams who I have worked with in a myriad of primary schools across this country and internationally. I would particularly like to thank Helen Robinson who has given me access to her wonderful school in Quarry Bank in the West Midlands to work with staff across the school in pursuit of how theory plays out in practice. Another inspiration is my friend Carol Aston whose love of learning and particularly literacy as the key to unlocking potential has inspired me with her expertise and enthusiasm. Geralyn Wilson has been with me on an educational journey and deep friendship for over 40 years and her experience as a headteacher and leader in education have helped me enormously. Family continue to be the rock that creates the strength and determination to see any project through and that is certainly true of mine. My daughter Rebecca is an inspiration, my stepsons James and William, my son in law Thomas and my husband Graham are all wonderful. My grandchildren, Alfred and Flora, are both now at school and it is to them that I want to dedicate this book. Harry and Roxy are not far behind. If we create for all children a love of learning and the desire to seek and find out more it will sustain them for their own journey through life. Lastly but by no means least I would like to say thank you to Diana Alves from Sage who has been with me through the development of this book. Her patience and positive feedback have kept me writing from the very first chapter to the end.

1

THE CURRICULUM AS THE FULCRUM FOR LEARNING AND ACHIEVEMENT – A REVIEW OF THE PAST TEN YEARS

A curriculum is the knowledge, skills and attributes that are required for educating individuals to be participants in a complex and pluralistic modern society. (*The Dictionary of Education*, Rowntree, 1981, a definition of curriculum)

What is a curriculum?

The curriculum is an essential part of the jigsaw that is the primary school. However, what it is and means to ensure all pupils can emerge from their primary journey achieving their full potential has proven difficult to quantify by successive governments and policy-makers.

A curriculum exists to change the pupil, to give the pupil new power. One acid test for a curriculum is whether it enables even lower-attaining or disadvantaged pupils to clamber in to the discourse and practices of educated people, so that they gain the powers of the powerful. (Counsell, 2018)

Reviewing the primary curriculum in the late 2000s

There have been many attempts at reform of the curriculum. Two significant pieces of research were an integral part of the latter years of the Blair/Brown governments before 2010. The Rose Review, commissioned in January 2008, made recommendations with regard to curriculum reform detailing six areas of learning:

- Understanding English, communication and languages
- Mathematical understanding
- Scientific and technological understanding
- Human, social and environmental understanding
- Understanding physical health and well-being
- Understanding the arts and design.

There was also the Cambridge Primary Review (Alexander, 2009) which was first commissioned in 2006 and was entitled *The Condition and Future of Primary Education*. This review looked in detail at what was positive and what their research suggested needed to be changed. In terms of curriculum, they wanted to see eight domains or priorities:

- Equity for all
- Learner voice
- Community engagement
- Sustainability and global citizenship
- Aims and a coherent vision for 21st-century primary education

- A broad, balanced and rich curriculum
- A pedagogy of repertoire, rigour, evidence and principle
- Assessment to enhance learning.

The Cambridge review provides within it an overview of the main changes since 1944 when the Butler Education Act enshrined primary education in law (Alexander, 2009). Looking at the list of reforms since then, one would be forgiven for thinking that not much has changed in the continued debate as to what the curriculum is, what it should include and how far reaching is its remit in shaping policy and practice in the primary school. We can go back even further:

> The mode of teaching in the primary schools has certainly fallen off in intelligence, spirit and inventiveness. It could not well be otherwise … in a country where everyone is prone to rely too much on mechanical processes and too little on intelligence. (Arnold, 1867)

A quote from Matthew Arnold, School Inspector (1867), reinforces the dilemma between autonomy and prescription. Mechanical processes might not be the issue in the 21st century but a snapshot of data linked to a narrow set of tests at the end of both primary stages does dampen for many primary school teachers their potential towards spirit and inventiveness and evidence of depth and breadth of expertise in their chosen subject.

Robin Alexander and his team at the University of Cambridge saw their opportunity to focus on far-reaching reform and a complete change of emphasis for the future of primary education in England. They made recommendations about the system, the starting age, broadening the curriculum, teaching methodologies and reform of the SEND agenda. The timing of the report was unfortunate for them as by the time they were launching their proposals in a series of conferences and press releases, a new government and new political thinking was about to be the dominant part of a new coalition government.

A change of regime and a change of policy

The new coalition government from 2010 set about creating their brand of education and in particular curriculum reform with the explicit aim of reducing central prescription. A suite of reviews set the process in motion. The National Curriculum Review published in 2011 and chaired by Tim Oates drew upon international research and the need to include an explicit remit explained at the beginning of the review, that the National Curriculum is developed in line with the principles of freedom, responsibility and fairness. Therefore the curriculum programmes of study should set out only essential knowledge and provide enough scope for schools to develop more locally relevant curricula linked to the needs of pupils and the particular setting the school represents (Oates, 2011).

Two other reviews, both published in 2011, also informed decisions made about the soon to be published National Curriculum:

- The Tickell Review – The Early Years: Foundations for Life, Health and Learning (Tickell, 2011)
- Lord Bew's Independent Review of Key Stage 2 Testing, Assessment and Accountability (Bew, 2011)

Drawing on the findings of these reviews and other research undertaken by the DfE, the then Education Secretary Michael Gove launched the content of England's revised National Curriculum a year later in 2012. Gove's wish to focus on a decluttering of content that created more autonomy in curriculum making was clear in the shaping of the foundation subjects. However, as for the core subjects, the prescription as to what and how they should be taught allowed for little or no autonomy. The new curriculum was criticised for being short on aims and a lack of balance.

> Since this contrast is reinforced by assessment requirements, with English, mathematics and science subject to national tests and 'some form of grading of pupil attainment', we can be reasonably sure on the basis of past experience that in a significant proportion of schools teachers will teach to the test and have scant regard for the rest. (Robin Alexander, author of the Cambridge Primary Review commentating in 2012)

2014, a new National Curriculum and an end to a long-established grading system

The new National Curriculum was first used in schools in September 2014. It came into being at the same time as a complete reform of assessment methodologies. The National Curriculum Review took account of respondents who replied to the review's call for evidence and what was said in the Bew review of primary testing, assessment and accountability to discontinue the use of prescribed levels of progression. For several years assessment was determined for educators with a set of grades. These were progressive from level 1 to level 8 where level 1 is low, and level 8 is high. The criteria and level descriptors were very clearly set out. The teacher benchmarked their assessment of where a pupil was along the scale. This provided the teacher with an assessment framework that was consistent across their school and also consistent across the whole country. The criticism of this approach was that it led to a lack of positive and deeply constructive feedback that would support how well the learner understood their own role in moving to the next level or sub-level. It was also observed that pupils would often only be interested in their grade and not how they could improve or understand what they had learnt.

A Commission on Assessment without Levels was appointed. They produced a 54-page guidance document to support teachers to understand what this change would mean in terms of their approach to assessment of pupils' work across all subjects. Levels went, and nothing replaced them except for a section in the Commission's guidance focusing on the principles of in-school formative and summative assessment. The following quote from the report illuminates the message to all in education that schools were in control of determining what and how to assess pupils' progress, their grasp of knowledge and their acquisition of skills.

> There is no 'one-size fits all' system for assessment. The best forms of in-school formative and summative assessment will be tailored to the school's own curriculum and the needs of the pupils, parents and staff. (Commission on Assessment without Levels, p. 24)

It therefore falls to the school to use what is an established system that has been with us for over sixty years. Assessment of learning and the cognitive processes involved in deepening understanding and mastery of learning are definitely the domain of the original Bloom's Taxonomy first defined in 1956. Bloom was one of several academics involved in the final taxonomy but as he was leading the project, his name has defined it, by default. His taxonomy is a ladder of nouns that start at the bottom of the list with knowledge and end at the top with evaluation:

- Evaluation
- Synthesis
- Analysis
- Application
- Comprehension
- Knowledge

A revision of Bloom's original taxonomy was published in 2001 by two academics: Lorin Anderson and David Krathwohl. It is this model that current thinking relies upon. Their interpretation of the original uses verbs instead of nouns and changes the order slightly. Their taxonomy starts at the bottom of the list with 'to remember' and ends at the top with 'to create':

- Create
- Evaluate
- Analyse
- Apply
- Understand
- Remember

Ultimately their explanation of the purpose of the new taxonomy (Anderson and Krathwohl, 2001) is to focus on four different types and levels of knowledge: factual, conceptual, procedural and metacognitive. The verbs provide an opportunity for the teacher to assess themselves in relation to both teaching subject knowledge and supporting pupils in enhancing their ability to think deeply, analyse, synthesise and ultimately use their learning to produce or generate ideas or create something new or different. This taxonomy links to the ladder of learning that exists within the programmes of study for maths, English and science where there is a clear progression from Early Years to Year 6 that focuses on increased cognitive demand in relation to knowledge pupils will acquire, how they build on that knowledge over time and how they make connections, compare and contrast, apply, explain, make patterns or develop conceptual understanding.

'Remember' is an interesting first step in this new taxonomy. Knowledge entering the long-term memory is a prerequisite that learning has taken place and therefore may place it further along the taxonomy. Maybe a better term would be 'recall' as to learn the fundamentals requires much practice and rote learning such as learning times tables, turning the alphabet into words and meaning and knowing how to use number to make sense of the world. This learning begins with early years and Key Stage 1 where learners learn the basics through recall and practice. This is where they develop their skills, ready for deeper curriculum enquiry and the acquisition of knowledge and more competent use of their skills. In a similar way in order to describe the pupil has to have the vocabulary and knowledge to demonstrate their understanding.

In the main this new taxonomy creates a powerful opportunity to focus on what these verbs mean in relation to teaching, learning and assessment. All teachers both new and experienced need the opportunity to explore the depth to which they need to plan for challenge, define the vocabulary and build opportunities for deep learning to take place. It is a challenge and requires a systematic focus on policy and implementation that is consistent across the whole school.

The lack of a framework of grade descriptors, such as the levels that defined the previous system, for teachers to use has meant that all schools have had to define their own rubric to assess where pupils are along a progressive spectrum from emerging to exceeding or with the use of similar terms (see Table 1.1).

Table 1.1 Rubrics to support progression – a few examples from different primary schools

Emerging	Achieving	Exceeding
Beginning	Developing	Secure
Beginning	Capable	Accomplished
Where now?	Where else?	Where next?

Curriculum change for core learning and autonomy for the foundation subjects

The core curriculum was set out in detailed programmes of study (DfE, 2014) with very prescriptive outcomes clearly outlined. Conversely vague, intended to be autonomous, programmes of study for all the other foundation subjects were published, ready to be taught as part of the curriculum offer across all primary schools in England. The prescription was in the delivery of a suite of foundation subjects and not in how or what was to be taught. However, there was also a requirement to teach SMSC, RE and Citizenship including British Values. Suddenly the primary curriculum became very crowded, especially if the timetable interpreted the delivery of the National Curriculum as a series on unrelated and unconnected subjects.

The main changes to the curriculum in terms of the core were far-reaching and remain a challenge for many who are charged with designing the primary curriculum.

The English programme of study for Key Stage 2 is now deeply grammar centric. It requires pupils and their teachers to have a command of the English language that is theoretical (DfE Programme of Study for English KS1 and 2). The consequence in the early days of the new curriculum meant that many pupils were taught the language of grammar rather than the flow of how to write for pleasure, to share information or ideas, or to find a solution. Grammar in its purest form was the subject to be taught. This is evident in the 24-page appendix to the English programme of study (DfE, 2014).

In maths what had been taught in Year 6 was now taught in Year 4 with the inevitable consequence that the curriculum in maths had to undergo considerable change with regard to how it was delivered in Key Stage 1 and lower Key Stage 2. Essentially this meant that in upper Key Stage 2 leading towards SATs in the spring of Year 6 learners were learning maths that would have previously been taught in early Key Stage 3. It is acknowledged by many commentators that there was an imperative to focus on this shift in the curriculum and effectively teach to the test in upper Key Stage 2 in order that both learners and teachers would be ready for the more difficult SATs papers. How long for was not discussed and maths remains a subject where teachers feel they have to teach to the test.

Science also changed. The emphasis changed from 'How Science Works' to 'Thinking and Working Scientifically'. For many this was a difficult leap. Finding scientists who want to teach in the primary sector has always been problematic, so it is often taught by non-specialists. The shift to thinking scientifically does suggest that some background in science is an essential prerequisite for the school staff responsible for developing a science curriculum; they do need to demonstrate that they have the training that allows them to think scientifically and work scientifically.

Science remains an issue for many in the primary phase. However, there is no SATs test to undergo, just a possibility that individual schools will be singled out for a random review of work completed by learners in Year 6.

Data and accountability

Where data drives accountability it is understandable that school leaders and their senior teams are compelled to ensure that pupils are equipped with the necessary skills and knowledge to pass the tests imposed upon them.

During Key Stage 2, following the introduction of the new National Curriculum the curriculum inevitably narrowed for some pupils. Headteachers across the primary sector felt the pressure on them to plan the curriculum in such a way as to ensure a large enough cohort of their pupils achieved sufficiently well in their end of Year 6 tests.

> In year five we have a reduced number of foundation subjects on the curriculum and in year six we focus almost exclusively on the teaching of Maths and English so that our pupils have the best possible chance in their SATs tests. (Phase leader for Upper Key Stage 2 from a school in Bolton in 2015)

There was to some extent a confusion, a contradiction created through the lack of balance in the emphasis the core created. On the one hand the Department for Education's policy was to create a knowledge-focused curriculum that gave teachers autonomy over what they taught. On the other hand the same teachers had their hands tied behind their backs because they were compelled to prepare their pupils for narrow but highly significant end-of-phase tests. These tests at the end of Key Stage 1 and 2 were to provide junior and secondary phase leaders with a set of data that would provide a flight path for each individual child. In other words, their performance in a test at the end of Key Stage 1 or Key Stage 2 would provide a clear trajectory of where they should be by the end of the next phase of learning. This approach clearly does not consider any of the bumps in the road that many pupils could face – loss, illness, moving school or the myriad of other obstacles that are part of growing up. This was all before the potentially catastrophic impact of the pandemic on learning and well-being.

The picture of pupils being taught to the test for months on end was easy to formulate for any observer visiting a school, particularly where they were invited into a Year 6 class. The consequence was more disturbing. Many secondary schools were now in a position of having to trust a data set that was arrived at through the 'spoon-feeding' of pupils in elements of the English, maths and science curricula. They also in some instances had to fill the gaps for many pupils who had not received any subject-specific teaching or learning for up to a year.

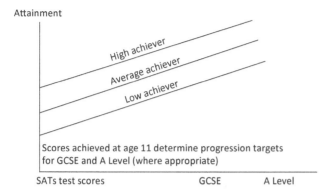

Figure 1.1 The flight path of accountability and progression

Change was inevitable

Many school leaders and their teams as well as teachers and their representatives were beginning, by the end of 2016, to question these ambiguities. Narrowing the curriculum in this way has led many to pose questions about the efficacy of the policy and a need to think again about what the curriculum is for and how it should be taught.

A new Ofsted Chief Inspector, Amanda Spielman, appointed in 2017, was the catalyst for change. She immediately began to challenge the obvious consequence of this imbalance in the way the curriculum was being delivered at both Key Stage 2 and 3 and through her appearance at several high-profile conferences announced her intention to make changes, not to the National Curriculum itself, but as to how it should be planned, implemented and assessed.

> Too many teachers and leaders have not been trained to think deeply about what they want their pupils to learn and how they are going to teach it. We saw curriculum narrowing, especially in upper key stage 2, with lessons disproportionately focused on English and mathematics. Sometimes, this manifested as intensive, even obsessive, test preparation for key stage 2 SATs that in some cases started at Christmas in Year 6. (Amanda Spielman, September 2018)

She also began a consultation process to look at the re-design of the Ofsted Handbook for Schools. Her focus, the quality of education and creating for schools an imperative to concentrate on how the curriculum ensures depth and breadth and parity for all learners whatever their starting point. From her speeches and obvious determination to make changes, she was clearly aware that the consequences of the dichotomy between ensuring high levels of success in core subjects at the end of Key Stage 1 and 2 and the lack of emphasis on accountability in non-core or foundation subjects was narrowing the curriculum offer significantly and leaving many pupils without a broad body of knowledge and vocabulary that they would need for the next stage of their education.

Spielman began to use three words to specify her desire to put the curriculum at the heart of creating high quality education outcomes for all. Intent, Implementation and Impact were to be the mantra for curriculum design and delivery.

Redressing the balance

Spielman's determination to make changes was underpinned by the commissioning of a series of pieces of research. The first piece of research asks some searching questions:

- What do we understand to be the real substance of education?
- What is the role of the school leader?
- How important are teachers as creators of excellence in pedagogy for learning?
- How do we make the right choices about what we teach the next generation?

As part of the commentary on this first piece of research Ofsted asks the questions above. Spielman is categorical in her belief that:

> Without a curriculum, a building full of teachers, leaders and pupils is not a school. Without receiving knowledge, pupils have learned nothing, and no progress has been made – whatever the measures might indicate. This is why exams should exist in the service of the curriculum rather than the other way round. Exams are our best measure of what has been successfully transmitted to the pupil's cognition. We must not forget, however, that any test can only ever sample the knowledge that has been gained. It is the whole domain that is of matter to the pupil. (Amanda Spielman, 2018)

The sample is very small, which has drawn some criticism. However, some interesting conclusions were made following this first piece of research.

- Even though the curriculum is what is taught, there is little debate or reflection about it
- School leaders discussed the timetable, which is not the curriculum
- Apart from the timetable, there was an absence of other tangible reference points to get to grips with the complex business of curriculum planning
- A lack of clarity around the language of the curriculum meant that the use of specific curriculum-related terms were woolly such as skills, progression, enrichment, questioning, repetition

The conclusion drawn from these observations was that the findings expose a weak theoretical understanding of curriculum planning. The reason cited was that in the past trainee teachers were taught the theory of curriculum planning but over time this fell away because of the introduction of a National Curriculum.

The report suggests that the overarching consequence of the findings for primary schools was how difficult they found recruiting staff who could design a curriculum. The suggestions were, as previously observed, that trainee teachers were learning how to teach to the English and mathematics tests with little attention given to developing deeper into curriculum knowledge. CPD to address this, according to some head-teachers, was difficult to access due to funding and a lack of local authority support.

This first piece of research certainly reinforced the perception that teaching to the test was at the heart of curriculum planning and led to a significant narrowing of the wider curriculum specifically in the foundation subjects. The introduction of tougher assessment criteria for new SATs was the essential priority for any staff training at the expense of wider curriculum development and planning.

Re-vitalising curriculum thinking

The second phase of Ofsted's research into curriculum design was published in the summer of 2018. Its purpose was to look at a group of high-performing schools which were 'invested in curriculum development and thinking' (Ofsted, 2018). The study was looking to identify common factors associated with schools which were committed to positive curriculum development.

Within this very small study of some good and outstanding schools the findings indicated three different approaches.

- Firstly were schools whose curriculum was knowledge rich. These schools see the important element of curriculum implementation to be the mastery of a body of knowledge. The skills are seen as an outcome of the curriculum, not its purpose
- A second group of schools took a knowledge-engaged approach. This is where knowledge enables the application of skills where skills are taught alongside knowledge
- The third group of schools, the smallest of the sample, demonstrate that they had a skills-led curriculum. Here schools designed their curriculum around skills that pupils need for future learning

With such a small sample it is difficult to draw a conclusion as to the efficacy of any of the above approaches to curriculum design. However, it is my assertion that younger learners in early years and Key Stage 1 will essentially be taught using a skills-led curriculum model. Children of this age are learning the basics, developing their understanding of the world through learning their letters and how they form words and their numbers as a starting point for developing skills as mathematicians. They may use knowledge as an essential element within their learning but the skills are the main focus. See the quote below taken from the Executive Summary in the National Curriculum Review (2011) where the discussion is about knowledge and development.

> The two elements (knowledge and development) are not, however, equally significant at every age. In particular, developmental aspects and basic skills are more crucial for young children, while appropriate understanding of more differentiated subject knowledge, concepts and skills becomes more important for older pupils.

In Key Stages 2 and 3 learners must have the basic skills in order that they can read and access knowledge in a range of both core and foundation subjects, write and demonstrate their understanding and use their oracy skills to explain, argue and debate the knowledge they are retaining. Therefore the curriculum is essentially knowledge-engaged.

When learners begin their Key Stage 4 journey it is presumed that most will have the skills they need to access knowledge at a higher level and that they have become unconsciously competent in their use of the skills they need for learning. With this in mind the curriculum makers can begin to formulate a more knowledge-led curriculum.

For those involved in curriculum design a sound understanding of all three of these approaches will provide the basis for making sound judgements as to the ambition the school has for its learners in defining the curriculum vision and intent. Where learners in Key Stage 2 have not grasped the basics, it is fair to suggest that the curriculum offered to them is skills-led to fill the gaps. This approach must provide the evidence that the curriculum design has parity for all learners and recognises that learners have different starting points.

Aiming for a knowledge-engaged model in Key Stage 2 would be my favoured approach to ensuring that all learners can begin to use their skills, especially those taught in English and mathematics, as part of developing complex and deep understanding in science and across the whole spectrum of foundation subjects. This is highlighted where we focus on the essential skill of reading that must be at the heart of learning in all subjects. This combined with a focus on rich and complex vocabulary defined for all subjects where there is explicit teaching of root words, definitions and anomalies will help all learners to read with confidence and comprehension.

The findings of this phase 2 research highlight that most curriculum leaders surveyed stressed the need to focus on the local context and highlighted the necessity to make sure that where knowledge and skills were not developed at home they should be developed in school, which again suggests that a differentiated model where a skills-led and knowledge-engaged approach will both be essential as part of curriculum design in most primary schools.

Two other points that came out of this phase of research are, firstly, the importance of regular reviews where progression was a key component. Most said they had subject-specific progression models in place that focus on progression through the content to be learned and this appeared to aid curriculum thinking. Therefore the curriculum is the progression model. Secondly, to ensure sustainability there is an imperative to ensure that the leadership of the curriculum is distributed, as when the headteacher is the sole source of curriculum thinking it can be hard to sustain.

Intent into implementation

Following on from phase 2 of their research programme Ofsted began to ask the question:

'Are intentions being followed through into implementation?' (Ofsted, 2018)

Ofsted's third piece of research wanted to test a model of inspecting how the curriculum is taught, subsequent pupil outcomes and the consistency across the school. Based on their phase 2 findings, Ofsted wanted to determine how to collect valid evidence on curriculum intent and implementation to form a broader quality of education judgement for their soon to be published inspection framework to be used from September 2019.

The sample comprised 64 schools of which 33 were primary schools and two were special schools. The schools were selected to reflect a diverse range in terms of inspection grades, attainment, type and demographic. At this point there emerged a suite of 25 curriculum indicators that would underpin what they were looking for in terms of the quality of education judgement in the then draft inspection handbook.

The research used visits to schools to look at:

- Their unique curriculum offer
- How well the curriculum was implemented in partnership with and alongside school staff
- The impact on the deliberate actions of leaders to implement their curriculum
- To look at first-hand evidence of curriculum planning
- To look at a curriculum journey that pupils would undertake from their first year to their final year in school

The findings in the primary schools highlighted some of those from phase 1 of their research. Some schools have an imbalanced curriculum offer which is not as challenging as that set out in the National Curriculum of 2014. They found that the structure and timetabling of the school day in some cases further limited curriculum development across subjects. In many examples the curriculum was being delivered much more effectively and with wider coverage in the core subjects than in the foundation subjects.

Also, in relation to subject knowledge, many teachers in the primary phase did not have the necessary skills or expertise to teach all the foundation subjects. It was found that there needed to much more in the way of CPD for early career teachers and for teachers who were teaching subjects they were not trained for. There was also evidence that there were fewer opportunities for professional development in the foundation subjects. There was some evidence that CPD was concentrated on training in the teaching of maths and English.

There was positive evidence that leaders ensure that the curriculum is appropriate to the context of the school and meets the particular aims and values of their school. There was also evidence that leaders understood the way in which knowledge is acquired and that it is generative. They knew how progression can be clearly planned in subjects but there seemed some issue with the fact that this does not always translate into subject-level implementation.

A clear finding – and one that we shall explore in more detail in Chapter 2 – is the important and central role of leadership in both curriculum development and accountability. The report highlights the need for leaders to ensure that the curriculum is prioritised so that the planned curriculum is implemented successfully across a wide range of subjects ensuring high-quality outcomes. Effective leadership, the report continues, needs the language and understanding of curriculum coherence, a key factor in curriculum effectiveness. Furthermore, they say, there is a strength in how subject and curriculum leaders are held to account for checking the depth and coverage of knowledge that is taught and the progression learners make.

The issue of subject-specific knowledge and the lack of professional development for both school leaders and their subject specialists was highlighted. Effective school leaders, they say, must have a solid understanding of the requirements of curriculum subjects, including the full component parts of each subject discipline. Also, they must ensure that middle leaders and teachers access specialist help and advice so that the curriculum is planned and taught well.

> Teachers have good knowledge of subject(s) and courses they teach. Leaders provide effective support for those teaching outside their main areas of expertise. (Ofsted grade description for good in the Quality of Education section of their Inspection Framework)

Pedagogy and lesson observation

As we moved towards the summer of 2019 with a new inspection handbook for schools in England to be used from the September, Ofsted published another piece of research looking at pedagogy and lesson observation, pupil outcomes and the need for a focus on professional conversations and dialogue to ensure cohesion.

Firstly, they published a table of 18 indicators linked to what inspectors should be looking for in relation to curriculum, teaching and behaviour. This list of indicators was not intended as advice or guidance for school leaders and their teams but was to be used to test the efficacy of observation by inspectors. What should they be looking for and how accurately would different inspectors assess the same lesson? The indicators were used in several pilot schools and inspectors observed lessons in twos. Each inspector had the same rubric (see Table 1.2) to assess the lesson against. The scores could then be compared to see any similarities and differences in their respective assessment.

Whatever the original intention for these indicators they do provide something that school, curriculum and subject leaders can use to determine their own benchmarks for high-quality pedagogy in the classroom.

A list of indicators for inspectors to focus on lesson observation outcomes linked to curriculum included:

- Teachers use subject expertise, knowledge and practical skills to provide learning opportunities
- Teachers ensure there is an equality of opportunity for all learners to access every lesson, as building blocks to the wider curriculum
- Strategies to support reading/vocabulary understanding/numeracy are in place
- The content of the lesson is suitably demanding
- The lesson content is appropriate to the age group and does not lower expectations
- There is a logical sequence to the learning
- Teachers provide opportunities to recall and practise previously learned skills and knowledge
- Assessment provides relevant, clear and helpful information about the current skills and knowledge of learners

Work scrutiny and assessment

A second strand of this research links to the assessment of what learners produce. Ofsted used the word scrutiny and seemed at the time to want to include only the work found in books. Their research was limited to those subjects where it would be reasonable to suppose the pupils would be using books to record their learning. Clearly, from a school's perspective and from mine, work produced by learners covers a much wider focus than what is found in exercise books. In primary schools, there is an imperative to define the learning more widely by looking at many examples of successful learning outcomes, practical models, oral presentations, artwork, prowess on the sports field, musical performance, to name but a few.

This piece of research included a third element which gave it the status of a 'triangulation'. This was the imperative to make sure that curriculum designers, planners, teachers and their support teams talk to each other. This is not tested and there are no indicators or rubrics attached to it. It is, however, linked forever to the concept of 'the deep dive' questions that Ofsted subsequently defined as part of their preparation for inspections using the new Education Inspection Framework (EIF) first published in September 2019.

Creating a constancy of purposes

The purpose of this third element of the triangulation was to reinforce the message that creating high-quality education requires a constancy of purpose. In order to achieve this, evidence must show a deep understanding of what constitutes best practice and how this can be replicated and modelled. The 'deep dive' questions remain an attempt to create a collaborative and unified approach to curriculum implementation. Where all staff from across the learning spectrum work together to determine

Table 1.2 Indicators used by Ofsted to review accuracy of inspections by inspectors

Building on previous learning	Depth and breadth of coverage	Pupils' progress	Practice
Pupils' knowledge is consistently, coherently and logically sequenced so that it can develop incrementally over time. There is a progression from the simpler and/or more concrete concepts to the more complex and/or abstract ones. Pupils' work shows that they have developed their knowledge and skills over time.	The content of the tasks and pupils' work show that pupils learn a suitably broad range of topics within a subject. Tasks also allow pupils to deepen their knowledge of the subject by requiring thought on their part, understanding of subject-specific concepts and making connections to prior knowledge.	Pupils make strong progress from their starting points. They acquire knowledge and understanding appropriate to their starting points.	Pupils are regularly given opportunities to revisit and practice what they know to deepen and solidify their understanding in a discipline. They can recall information effectively, which shows that learning is durable. Any misconceptions are addressed and there is evidence to show that pupils have overcome these in future work.

what will be taught in relation to their subject and its place in the wider curriculum, there should be evidence of a collaborative approach to ensuring intent translates into positive implementation.

Measuring high-quality education was the essential change to the inspection framework in September 2019. It was made absolutely clear that the meaning of quality in this context was the curriculum and how well it was designed and delivered. The imperative was for school leaders to work together with their curriculum and subject teams to define quality in relation to their own vision for the school and ambition for learners. The paradigm shift from a real emphasis on summative data as the key driver of accountability had to be made. A broad range of subjects had to be taught. Subject experts had to be found. The decision as to what kind of curriculum to design, knowledge-led, knowledge-engaged or skills-led had to be decided upon. There was also a clear emphasis on focusing on the how to teach the concepts that transcend subjects such as equality, power, freedom and sustainability.

It was a crucial learning curve for most in the profession. Armed with the research and a wealth of resources from all sorts of different sources progress began to be made. The focus was on creating a deep and rich curriculum where the foundation subjects were an essential ingredient in developing the whole learner so that they will be equipped with the knowledge and skills ready for the next stage in their education.

And then came the pandemic

September 2019 to March 2020 saw many headteachers and their senior teams focusing on how to ensure their rationale and ambition for the curriculum and how it would support all learners was translated into good pedagogy and high-quality learning. CPD was a focus for those involved in planning for teaching the foundation subjects alongside continuing to teach high-quality lessons in maths, English and science.

The events that unfolded as the Covid-19 virus took hold were difficult to comprehend at first. The unbelievable news that schools would close for all but key workers' children took us all by surprise.

All those who are part of the teaching profession were heroic in how they rose to the challenge of continuing to educate pupils at home as well as for some still in school. Overcoming sometimes insurmountable obstacles, remote and blended learning began to emerge as the norm. Teachers learnt how to use Teams and Zoom. Children learnt how to manage their own time, find space to work and be resilient in situations where there was no teacher, no friends, no routine.

Several commentators have attempted to define the quality of learning and teaching during this time and, in particular, UNESCO's report From Disruption to Recovery (2020) and the Education Endowment Foundation (2020) have produced comprehensive research studies into the effects on learning, attainment and progression here in the UK and internationally. Phrases like 'catch-up' and 'lost learning' do not do justice to the hard work of parents, teachers, pupils and the wider community in creating a culture where learning for many did continue.

The opportunities to refocus on the curriculum as the fulcrum for managing the way out of an extraordinary period in history must not be lost. There is an imperative to reshape the learning and develop creative solutions to how to fill the gaps in learning for some, reassure those who are less confident and capitalise on new ways to use technology in building new futures for the rest of the 21st century and beyond.

A crossroads in curriculum thinking

We are at a crossroads in curriculum thinking that still requires leaders to know what they want to achieve through the design and delivery of a creative, broad and knowledge-rich curriculum offer that inspires all pupils to want to learn. Dwelling on the past and on what has not been achieved will never work. Building curriculum strategies that focus on subject knowledge and the skills pupils need to make sense of that knowledge is essential. Recognising and capturing gaps in learning through this process will put things right far more quickly than trying to teach what has been lost before moving on to new learning. Where is the time, the energy and the motivation for that?

It has already been highlighted that the primary curriculum was in the throes of change by the end of 2019 and at the beginning of 2020. New approaches to ensuring depth and breadth in how the foundation subjects were taught and greater emphasis on learning the core through the development of deeper subject and conceptual knowledge was beginning to be an integral part of planning what would be taught.

The primary profession must look to what was the norm before the pandemic took us all by surprise and accept that we were only just beginning to focus on new ways to deliver the curriculum that ensured deeper learning for all. Looking back to the time before the new Education Inspection Framework and the strong focus on curriculum coherence, it is good to focus on the following questions:

- How much learning was lost when schools chose to emphasise the teaching of the core at the expense of the foundation subjects, particularly English and maths in year 6 in order to prepare pupils for SATs?
- How much learning was lost when pupils moved from one year to the next without the teacher having a clearly sequenced curriculum map to make sure that they could plan to build on prior learning and acknowledge any gaps in learning?
- How much learning was lost at times of transition from one key stage to the next where teachers were not building academic learning partnerships across a transition bridge?
- How much learning was lost when teachers were ill equipped with sufficient subject knowledge to teach foundation subjects to a deeper level?

The publication of a series of subject reviews by Ofsted (2021 and 2022) has created a rich vein of commentary on best practice in subject and knowledge delivery, the common thread through all of them being their focus on how knowledge is taught, either substantive knowledge or disciplinary knowledge. Essentially, substantive knowledge is the facts and disciplinary knowledge is the way it is taught and the evidence that leads to the understanding of a growing body of knowledge. The subject reviews emphasise the importance of ensuring all teachers have the expertise to teach to the required depth. There is clearly an emphasis on ensuring the planning of the curriculum at both key stages 1 and 2 focuses on the training needs of those with subject responsibility. Otherwise, it is unlikely that what is planned can be implemented without the relevant level of teacher subject expertise.

Also, the development of the Early Career Framework DfE to be used in schools from September 2021 will provide those who support new and recently qualified teachers to develop as highly effective teachers. One of the sections is devoted to curriculum.

There is also new guidance on teaching in the Early Years and Foundation stages (DfE, 2021) which is where the journey begins. A clear focus on six key areas of development provide those with responsibility for the primary curriculum to plan with their early years colleagues to ensure a positive foundation for each pupil and an opportunity to ensure that all those who teach beyond this phase understand how they are building on prior learning and can use the skills and knowledge already embedded to build a sequence of learning.

The emphasis on a knowledge-led curriculum seems to be still very much at the heart of government policy in England and several high-level speeches from Nick Gibb and others confirm this highly contentious theory. His evidence is selective and lacks detail. There remain many unanswered questions about how we ensure a new dawn for the curriculum creates the right strategy for planning a sustainable future of learning.

Conclusion

This chapter focused on the major changes that have shaped educational thinking over the last decade and beyond. What has emerged during the past few years is a much greater emphasis on the curriculum and what should be taught in an ever-changing world where technology drives our economy and our futures.

Politics plays its part in how education is delivered. Most certainly this is evident from the account of policy, accountability, curriculum and assessment decisions that have shaped the changes documented here. It is, however, essential to know and understand what has gone before, and why in order to make decisions as to how to design and deliver a curriculum that meets the statutory requirements of the National Curriculum (DfE, 2014) while creating a model that will provide the best possible education that is relevant and inspirational for pupils within a specific local context.

Reading extensively has led me to the conclusion that although the emphasis changes regarding the theory of curriculum design at the school level the same key principles apply whatever regime sets the bar. Subject knowledge is an excellent starting point in conjunction with which subjects to emphasise and why. Knowing what content to include provides the opportunity to explain the rationale for the choices and why the inclusion of a range of specific topics and ideas demonstrates the ambition the school has for all of its pupils. Confidently outlining the key components of the knowledge pupils will gain over time creates the language of intent.

Implementation is a bit more complicated and is where positive leadership of the curriculum is essential. It is here that the architect of the curriculum must have a repertoire of key indicators of how subject knowledge will be delivered. There is the absolute importance of pedagogy and how the teacher ensures pupils develop the skills and behaviours they need to be successful at learning. There is an imperative to build on prior learning, focus on sequencing the learning over time and having expertise in how assessment leads to breadth, depth and positive progression. The task of creating the right culture that ensures all of these aspects of delivering a cohesive and all-embracing curriculum is an essential element of positive devolved leadership.

The following chapters look in detail at how primary school leaders and their teams can shape the future so that all pupils achieve their full potential and have the advantage of a rich, broad and deep curriculum that equips them with all they will need to be successful citizens where their dreams and aspirations can be realised. The collective experience of myself and my colleagues at Learning Cultures gives me an opportunity to share knowledge, deep research and a wealth of resources and materials that have successfully supported hundreds of senior and middle leaders as well as teachers and support staff to design and deliver outstanding education that inspires learning and has a profound impact on pupils and on continuing professional development for all those who work with them.

Top tips

- Although they are out of favour at the moment do have a look at the Cambridge Primary Review's eight domains – they are remarkably similar to many more recent commentaries.
- Review the programmes of study for English, maths and science in relation to key concepts that underpin learning in the foundation subjects.
- Revisit Anderson and Krathwohl's revised taxonomy and discuss with colleagues how the main components match your own current rubric for assessment.
- Review your current published curriculum intent in relation to how your curriculum rationale fits in with one or a combination of knowledge-led, knowledge-engaged or skills-led.
- Discuss with subject leaders and phase leaders the implication of a focus on one or more of the three approaches to curriculum design, i.e. knowledge-led, knowledge-engaged or skills-led, and which is best suited to pupils at different stages off their journey toward secondary school.
- Reflect with others about your strategy for reviewing how well learners are progressing and what steps are taken to close gaps in learning.
- Ask the question to yourself and to your senior and middle leadership teams, 'To what extent is the leadership of the curriculum distributed?'
- Work through the 25 curriculum indicators to establish where you are now, what is working well and what needs to change.
- Work with subject leaders to establish their interpretation of curriculum intent and how they are translating that into positive strategies for curriculum delivery.
- Ask all your staff to share their examples of positive outcomes that have emerged from the closure of schools in 2020 and 2021.

References

Alexander, R. (ed.) (2009) *Children, Their World, Their Education: Final Report and Recommendations of the Cambridge Primary Review*. London: Routledge.

Anderson, L. and Krathwohl, D. R. (eds) (2001) *A Taxonomy for Learning, Teaching and Assessing: A Revision of Bloom's Taxonomy of Educational Objectives*. New York: Longman.

Arnold, M. (1867) *Culture and Anarchy: An Essay in Political and Social Criticism*. London: Cornhill Magazine.

Bew, P. (2011) *Independent Review of Key Stage 2 Testing, Assessment and Accountability – Final Report*. London: DfE.

Counsell, C. (2018) 'Senior Curriculum Leadership 1: The indirect manifestation of knowledge: (B) final performance as deceiver and guide', *The dignity of the thing*, April 12, 2018 [Blog]. Available at: https://thedignityofthethingblog.wordpress.com/2018/04/12/senior-curriculum-leadership-1-the-indirect-manifestation-of-knowledge-b-final-performance-as-deceiver-and-guide/ (accessed 27 July 2022).

Department for Education (DfE) (2011) *The Framework for the National Curriculum. A Report by the Expert Panel for the National Curriculum Review*. London: DfE.

Department for Education (DfE) (2014) *National Curriculum in England: Framework for Key Stages 1 and 2*. London: DfE.

Department for Education (DfE) (2021) *Early Career Framework*. London: DfE.

Department for Education (DfE) (2021) *Statutory Framework for the Early Years Foundation Stage*. London: DfE.

Department for Education (DfE) and Standards and Testing Agency (2015) *Final Report of the Commission on Assessment without Levels*. London: DfE/Standards and Testing Agency.

Education Endowment Foundation (2020) *Covid-19 Support Guide for Schools*. London: Education Endowment Foundation.

Oates, T. (2011) *Cambridge Assessment National Curriculum Review Department of Education*.

Ofsted (2018) An Investigation Into How to Assess the Quality of Education Through Curriculum Intent, Implementation and Impact – Phase 3 Findings of Curriculum Research. Ofsted.

Ofsted (June 2019) *Research Commentary: Inspecting Education Quality – Lesson Observation and Workbook Scrutiny*. London: Ofsted.

Ofsted (July 2019) *Education Inspection Framework: Overview of Research*. London: Ofsted.

Ofsted (2021–2022) *Research Review Series: Science, RE, Maths, Languages, Geography, Music, History, PE, Computing, English*. London: Ofsted.

Spielman, A. (2017) *Amanda Spielman's Speech at the ASCL Annual Conference 2017*. [Speech transcript] ASCL Conference, International Convention Centre, Birmingham. 10 March 2017. Available at: https://www.gov.uk/government/speeches/amanda-spielmans-speech-at-the-ascl-annual-conference (accessed 27 July 2022).

Spielman, A. (2018) *HMCI Commentary: Curriculum and the New Education Inspection Framework*. London: Ofsted.

Rose, J. (2008) *Independent Review of the Primary Curriculum: Final Report*. London: DCSF.

Tickell, C. (2011) *The Early Years: Foundations for Life, Health and Learning*. London: DfE.

UNESCO (2020) *Education: From Disruption to Recovery*. Paris: UNESCO.

2

CURRICULUM INTENT, IMPLEMENTATION AND IMPACT – CREATING A WHOLE-SCHOOL SYNERGY

Effective leaders have a clear vision for the school – drawing on evidence – which is understood, owned, and implemented by all staff.

The best leaders make sure that this vision is driving all the decisions in the school, including how to teach and develop teaching, how to use resources effectively and how to organise their school so that teachers and pupils flourish.

(Effective primary teaching practice: Review by the Teaching Schools Council, 2016)

A changing world will need a dynamic curriculum

Change is a constant and ever so in education. The unprecedented events that led to school closures due to the worldwide Covid pandemic have meant that all of us in education have had to deal with even greater change and cope with challenges we could never have imagined. Much of what has taken place has given the profession positives as well as challenges and time to pause and rethink many of the processes and practices that we effectively took for granted previously.

The need for a dynamic and forward-thinking curriculum has never been more important. For all those involved in defining the curriculum content this is an exciting time. Pupils have lived through an extraordinary period in history and have had to face up to unprecedented change to their own lives. Incorporating this into the fabric of what will be learnt and how it will be taught and assessed should enrich the curriculum and provide pupils with the opportunity to make sense of their shared or very different experiences.

New approaches to teaching including blended and remote learning are likely to remain for some and provide a rich vein of scholarship that can only enhance what went before. Opportunities for enquiry, extended writing and the reading of rich texts is eminently more achievable through the infinite possibilities the internet gives us. Many who were perhaps unsure as to how to fully embrace technology as part of teaching and learning have had no choice and are now able to build new futures using the possibilities that remote and online learning bring with them.

Crafting the vision and rationale for a vibrant and energetic curriculum

Crafting the vision and rationale that accurately defines how each school's unique curriculum offer is ambitious, accessible and achievable is complex. It is important to contain the curriculum offer to within the boundaries of what can be achieved with limited resources and the potential lack of subject expertise. There are, however, limitless possibilities to be creative and innovative and to capture the enthusiasm of young learners and enrich the skills of the professionals who teach and support them along their primary journey (Priestley and Xenotantos, 2021).

A school is made up of a wealth of talent, often untapped and sometimes carefully hidden. A school leader or headteacher cannot be the sole architect of the school vision for curriculum excellence. There must a broad consensus that acknowledges the strengths within the school and that harnesses the potential where it is hidden or underused.

Senior leaders need the skills to build confidence and creativity within the teams that help to shape the curriculum and plan its implementation. Creating the right culture where staff feel empowered to innovate and use their expertise, qualifications or interests to help with the design of a creative curriculum can be highly motivating. Where staff share their strengths and know the gaps they have in their own knowledge there is a collective commitment to create something special and unique.

> What is clear is that leadership from the headteacher/principal and senior leadership team (SLT) is central both to curriculum development and accountability. Leaders in schools that prioritise the curriculum make it their business to ensure that the planned curriculum is implemented successfully across a wide range of subjects so that curriculum quality is high.
> (Commentary on phase 3 of Ofsted's research into curriculum design, January 2019)

Defining curriculum intent

Ofsted's original research into the quality of education was commissioned to explore curriculum design and therefore curriculum intent. It provides some scope for discussion as to the focus on what needs to be a part of the wider conversation for senior leaders: what should be included as an essential part of a curriculum and what is important for the school in relation to its own local and wider contexts. The research into curriculum design with its list of 25 indicators (discussed in Chapter 1) defines quite clearly what curriculum intent should include. Below are some questions that senior leaders must ask themselves and their teams as they look to shape meaningful statements of intent.

- What is the evidence that the curriculum rationale is carefully crafted to take account of the local context?
- How transparent and clear are the aims we have prescribed as essential for our curriculum?
- How are these aims communicated and shared across the school and fully understood by all?
- What is the evidence that the curriculum concepts used to define the vision and intent for curriculum design are understood by curriculum and subject leaders?
- What strategies have we used to make sure that curriculum coverage allows all pupils to access the content and make progress?

- What is the evidence that our planned curriculum content is ambitious and meets or exceeds the statutory national curriculum?
- How do we make sure literacy and reading is a key priority in every subject in both core and foundation subjects?
- How do we ensure that mathematical fluency is also a key priority and seen as an essential prerequisite for pupils to access the full curriculum offer?

The full set of 25 curriculum indicators that these questions are drawn from can be found in Ofsted's first phase of research into curriculum design (Ofsted, 2018).

Key concepts in curriculum design

Building a consensus on the blueprint or detailed architectural plan that defines the foundations of good curriculum design will be strengthened if there is also a consensus as to the key concepts that underpin the academic thinking behind its creation.

A concept is defined as 'a general idea or abstract notion'.

Concept in the context of curriculum design seems to be seen as the words and phrases that might help to explain to a stakeholder, implementer or inspector the true shape of the curriculum that will be taught and delivered. Research into others' views of concepts of curriculum design suggest that such words as depth, breadth, balance and relevance feature as well as essential building blocks of design such as the interweaving of discrete subjects, differentiation to match learning to pupil attainment and continuity that links existing knowledge with new knowledge. Using the term concept gives those with the role of deciding on its content and delivery models the autonomy to create a curriculum relevant to their cohort, the expertise of their staff and desire to create an offer that inspires, challenges and stretches all pupils to achieve their full potential. See Table 2.1 for a list of curriculum concepts that we have gathered from various representative groups, trade unions and subject associations, such as ASCL, ASE and The Key.

Table 2.1 Curriculum concepts gathered from various sources

• **Breadth** across a full range of subjects	• **Knowledge** linked to learning in and across subject divides
• **Balance** of time, subject content and skills development	• **Conceptual learning** applied in a variety of contexts across the curriculum
• **Relevance** to pupils' needs	• **Skills development** in relation to accessing learning, deepening learning and ensuring progression
• **Coherence** so that content inter-relates	
• **Interweaving** of discrete subjects	
• **Differentiation** to match learning to pupil attainment	• **Deepening understanding** to enable pupils to construct meaning
• **Progression** to extend learning, knowledge, skills and understanding	• **Attitudes** to learning and attitudes about learning
• **Continuity** that links existing with new subject knowledge	• **Subject vocabulary** is accessible and allows pupils to access knowledge

The explicit role of the senior leader in shaping the vision, the intent and the rationale

Designing a primary curriculum is complex. Senior leaders must gain the trust and confidence of all those who have the role of developing the subject-specific content across year groups, key stages and points of transition. The focus for the senior leader is to have the domain-specific knowledge that leads to deep educational expertise. This includes understanding the component parts of curriculum planning that will lead to high-quality outcomes for all pupils. The school leader must have a profound knowledge of pedagogy and what outstanding teaching looks like in the classroom. He or she must be clear as to how formative feedback and assessment lead to learning and progression. There must be a consensus as to what is meant by high-quality outcomes and explicit goals that define the impact the curriculum will have on pupil achievement, attainment and motivation.

> Leaders need to be increasingly knowledgeable about the core business of teaching, learning, assessment and curriculum. And they need to be able to use that knowledge to make good decisions.
>
> (Viviane Robinson speaking at The Ambition Institute in 2017)

The subject-specific detail does need to be left to the subject lead or expert. The headteacher will have knowledge of one or more subjects possibly from a previous role as a subject leader and from being a part of lesson observation and performance management, but an in-depth understanding of each subject is highly unlikely and unnecessary.

The role of the senior leader is therefore to:

- Set the strategic vision
- Create the right culture that ensures all pupils succeed
- Empower others to know their strengths and their needs and provide the resources to develop strong teams and individuals
- Develop staff so that they reach their full potential and have the pedagogical skills to share with their teams
- Build strong communities of practice that work together to deliver high-quality learning within subjects and across the curriculum
- Lead their teams in the pursuance of consistent and whole-school approaches to positive and progressive formative feedback
- Be able to accurately measure the impact of their subject leadership on school, team and individual success
- Create strategies that enable the gathering of evidence of where there are gaps in pupil learning and build a consensus as to how to ensure all pupils achieve their full potential

It is the role of the senior leadership team to pay attention to the school culture and community. There needs to be a consensus on their understanding of the nature and character of the pupils and their families, their environment, experiences and aspirations. This is an essential prerequisite to ensuring that the curriculum will link to a local context that all pupils can relate to as a starting point for learning. It is, however, essential that they can learn beyond the everyday. All pupils, whatever their starting point, deserve to have equality of opportunity and the chance to be amazed and curious in the pursuit of deep knowledge that widens their experiences and allows them to acquire a range of learning and life skills.

It is also important that the senior leader empowers all subject leaders or experts to ensure that their curriculum choices recognise pupils with SEND, pupils that need to be challenged, pupils that have few cultural experiences to draw on and those pupils who, for whatever reason, have gaps in their learning. Ensuring this philosophy is at the heart of the curriculum rationale and ambition is a truly inspirational starting point for subject experts and teachers.

Turning intent into implementation

There are many elements that need to be in place to turn the curriculum rationale and ambition for pupils into a reality. Senior leaders must take account of the resource implications, the close attention to mapping and sequencing that must take place and the depth to which the planned curriculum should reach in preparing pupils for the next stage in their education, the next year, the next phase or the next school.

The decision about what to teach and when to teach it is the domain of the subject expert. However, it is imperative that he or she can work in tandem with senior leaders to ensure that the curriculum vision is indeed translated effectively into subject specific learning. The focus on implementation must involve a shared commitment to:

- Ensuring all teachers have the expert subject knowledge of the subjects that they teach
- Creating opportunities for CPD to ensure gaps in subject knowledge for teachers are eliminated
- Ensuring teachers have a tacit understanding of the key concepts that are an essential component of their subject
- Understanding that some key concepts transcend other subjects and create opportunities for pupils to see connections and deepen their learning
- Understanding how teachers develop strategies that ensure learning is remembered and remains in the long-term memory
- Creating mechanisms that will allow knowledge and skills taught in one year to build on what has been taught before
- Knowing that the curriculum in all subjects follows a sequence so that learning deepens pupils' skills and knowledge over time
- Defining the end points pupils will reach as they journey through their time in primary school

- Identifying misconceptions, correcting them and then focusing on ensuring learners understand the curriculum that is taught to them
- Determining the strategies for formative assessment so that pupils can embed and use knowledge fluently to increase their understanding and make connections across many facets of their learning

The primary journey towards deep learning

Senior leaders in the primary sector must take a wide view of how the curriculum unfolds from Early Years to Year 6 to ensure pupils are fully equipped for the next stage of their education.

> Senior Leadership Teams need a curricular language for talking about teaching and attainment, a language which, because of its *curricular* character, illuminates rather than conceals the thing itself. Such a language cannot be empty of substance. It must be rooted in a shared knowledge base, one that makes curricular communication possible. (Christine Counsell, 2018)

Domain-specific knowledge will provide the senior leader with the ability to transcend subject-specific detail and build a consensus that subject-specific and cross-curricular planning dovetail into their explicit statement of intent, rationale and ambition for all pupils across the school. Senior leaders must know the questions to ask that will ensure they can see the bigger picture and be confident that explicit subject knowledge is closely linked to the aims defined in the National Curriculum programmes of study for each subject. The subject–specific detail is then the responsibility of the subject expert.

The aims within the English National Curriculum programme of study for Key Stage 1 and 2 are to ensure that all pupils (DfE, 2014):

- Read easily, fluently and with good understanding
- Develop the habit of reading widely and often, for both pleasure and information
- Acquire a wide vocabulary, an understanding of grammar and knowledge of linguistic conventions for reading, writing and spoken language
- Appreciate our rich and varied literary heritage
- Write clearly, accurately and coherently, adapting their language and style in and for a range of contexts, purposes and audiences
- Use discussion in order to learn: pupils should be able to elaborate and explain their understanding and ideas
- Are competent in the arts of speaking and listening, making formal presentations, demonstrating to others and participating in debate

Now look at the aims within the programme of study for Design Technology:

- Develop the creative, technical and practical expertise needed to perform everyday tasks confidently and to participate successfully in an increasingly technological world

- Build and apply a repertoire of knowledge, understanding and skills in order to design and make high-quality prototypes and products for a wide range of users
- Critique, evaluate and test their ideas and products and the work of others
- Understand and apply the principles of nutrition and learn how to cook

Words from the English programme of study such as fluently, accurately, coherently and elaborately and in the design technology programme of study build and apply, critique, evaluate and design and make all provide an opportunity to focus on how these words and phrases translate into high-quality pedagogy, skills competence, knowledge acquisition and positive pupil outputs. This pattern exists across all the programmes of study for Early Years and for Key Stage 1 and 2

The aims for each subject have a lot of generic similarities as well as subject-specific statements. This translates into the opportunity to focus on ongoing research by Ofsted into a review of subject-specific teaching. In each of the reviews (so far published up to December 2022) there is a clear distinction between substantive knowledge (the factual subject content) and disciplinary knowledge (the interconnected relationship between one area of learning and another) (see Table 2.2).

Table 2.2 The difference between substantive and disciplinary knowledge

Substantive knowledge	Disciplinary knowledge
<ul><li>Subject and factual content</li><li>The sequencing of the information</li><li>Essential subject knowledge</li><li>Subject rules and protocols</li><li>Layers of knowledge</li><li>Factual evidence</li><li>National Curriculum subject aims</li><li>Hierarchical structure</li></ul>	<ul><li>Making connections across a range of other subjects</li><li>Sharing ideas and different perspectives</li><li>Seeing the bigger picture</li><li>Making sense of the information</li><li>Comparing and contrasting with other facts and information</li></ul>

This body of research underpins the essential basis upon which the curriculum design and therefore intent is constructed to ensure that pupils have the core skills of literacy and numeracy firmly embedded in order that they can access the knowledge, make sense of it and make connections across all their learning.

Therefore the senior leader needs to have questions to hand that will provide subject leaders with the relevant challenge to ensure that the curriculum has breadth and balance. Senior leaders must be confident that implementation of the curriculum is a combination of skills development and the sequencing of subject knowledge over time.

Such questions might include:

- What through the teaching of your subject content inspires pupils to want to learn and find out more?
- How is learning differentiated to embrace the needs, experiences and aspirations of all pupils?

- What is the evidence that the planned curriculum builds on prior learning and is sequenced towards clearly defined end points?
- How are rich texts used to promote a growing confidence and love of reading across all subjects?
- Where do subject concepts transcend one subject and apply in the context of others?
- Where are there clearly stated opportunities to develop mathematical fluency where it is essential for the acquisition of knowledge in subjects other than maths?
- How can the defined curriculum content create for pupils an opportunity to recognise the generic and thinking skills that will allow them to access knowledge within and across all their learning?

Creating a coalition for learning and pedagogy

Deciding what to teach, in what order and to what depth are all part of defining the curriculum in terms of a school's desire to ensure all pupils achieve their full potential and leave at the end of Year 6 equipped with the skills and knowledge ready for the next stage of their education. Therefore it is essential that leaders of school, leaders of curriculum and leaders of subject-specific learning all work together to build a consensus of what the curriculum map looks like in relation to how learners build on prior learning, how well the learning is sequenced so that knowledge grows and the skills they need to access that knowledge develop over time. The curriculum blueprint ultimately needs to outline the plan for how all learners will make progress towards clearly defined end points at the end of topics, years and key stages.

Achieving the above can only be a reality if there are very clear strategies for collaboration and communication through creating opportunities for planning and learning collectively. Primary schools are made up of phases, key stages and year groups. Where the planning of the curriculum takes place within a year group or a phase it is unlikely that those planning for a different phase or year group will join up the curriculum thread that needs to be in place from early years to Year 6 and beyond.

There must be time and resources set aside to create for those who will be teaching the curriculum to work together to develop a sequential plan that shows clearly what will be taught in the Early Years Foundation Stage (EYFS), what is then taught in Key Stage 1 and how this is built on in lower and upper Key Stage 2. Those with real foresight will look to see what the secondary school would like pupils to know and be able to do by the time they are joining Year 7 and dovetail the learning so that pupils can indeed demonstrate to their Year 7 teachers that the learning they have undertaken along their primary journey has remained in their long-term memory.

Creating opportunities for teachers across the school to work together to plan their curriculum offer is CPD in itself. The coming together of individuals who have a wealth of knowledge, who have been educated to degree level and have various spans of teaching experience have the potential to be a huge force for creating powerful learning tools and strategies that will inspire learning both for the teachers and for the pupils. They need to focus on:

- Working collaboratively to build a continuum of learning from EYFS to Year 6 and beyond using the core and foundation programmes of study
- Examining the importance of literacy as the fulcrum for learning and knowledge acquisition in all subjects
- Sharing how numeracy is used to access knowledge and understanding in subjects other than maths
- Where subject concepts overlap how teachers can create a deeper understanding of what these mean in different subjects to help learners to make all important connections
- Helping pupils to know how they learn and how teachers can support them to deepen their knowledge so that it is retained in their long-term memory
- Creating an approach to formative assessment that involves the pupil and creates for all those involved with opportunities to see the learning, the gaps and misconceptions and where assessment is seen as an integral part of the learning process

Subjects are not single silos of learning. They interweave together and provide for the pupil opportunities to broaden their understanding and deepen their learning. It is therefore essential that curriculum planning looks beyond subject knowledge and defines the key concepts that may transcend the subject and help to create opportunities for pupils to make connections across the subject divides. Such concepts as settlement, power, equality, force all transcend subject divides and create a rich vein of pedagogy that can result in opportunities for pupils to reason, apply, express viewpoints, consider different opinions and understand the importance of evidence.

Figure 2.1 shows one possible way of organising working parties to work collectively to plan for more than one year together thus creating clear evidence that the curriculum being taught does recognise and build on what has been taught in previous years. The essential glue that knits this diagram together is the word transition. Where for instance teams from Year 1 and 2 work in tandem there needs to be opportunities for those involved in planning for Year 3 and 4 to be clear as to the content of the curriculum being taught in the infant phase. The strategic planning behind this process must define who is responsible for creating those communication channels across the key stages, phases and year groups.

This is a starting point for subject leaders and their teams to work collaboratively but requires in-depth thinking to create the culture that will deliver the curriculum intent that in some schools remains an aspiration and not a reality. The commitment of time for planning, for ongoing collaborative conversations and opportunities for reflection and review are a critical first step. Curriculum intent will be just that unless there is a strategic approach to building a consensus for how the curriculum will be delivered.

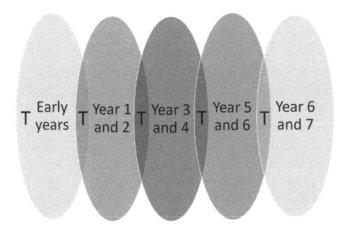

T = Transition – ensuring collaboration across the key stages

Figure 2.1 Creating a continuum of learning

Leadership cohesion will translate into curriculum cohesion

Making the decision to create the discussions and shared planning where senior leaders provide the time and resources for subject and curriculum leaders to work together is a powerful first step. The focus on a collaborative plan for curriculum implementation carefully crafted to meet the school vision and ambition will create profound evidence that there is cohesion and a shared commitment to ensuring high-quality education is a goal for all (Hargreaves and O'Conner, 2018).

For the senior leader the aims within the National Curriculum programmes of study (DfE, 2014) should suffice in terms of their understanding of the wider picture. The programmes of study also provide for the subject leader an opportunity to focus on reinforcement, acceleration and enrichment within the context of their own subject and across other subjects. For some the planning might require looking at the corresponding standard from the next year group or the one before or where the same standard is used in a different or unfamiliar context.

Planning how to teach the content requires the wider involvement of the teams that will deliver the curriculum. Their contribution to the planning process can be invaluable and where there are opportunities to create cross-curricular as well as subject-specific discussions teachers learn much about their own subject where there are links with other subjects and ideas. Creating opportunities to share pedagogical practice in how specific subject or conceptual knowledge is taught is invaluable. Where teachers work together within and across subject divides there are opportunities for an in-depth focus on how what is being taught in one subject may have relevance in another, certainly where skills and concepts are an essential part of the planning. We will examine this in more detail in the next three chapters.

There is also an imperative to ensure that assessment of the learning is seen as an integral part of this planning process. What pupils must achieve transcends the subject-specific content and includes the assessment of literacy and numeracy skills and the wider thinking skills that are integral across all subjects and provide for the pupil an opportunity to make connections across their learning and recognise that skills, most conspicuously literacy and numeracy skills, apply in all subjects. Raising awareness of this provides for the pupil an opportunity to move towards conscious and unconscious competence in their use of a range of powerful life skills. Chapter 7 looks in detail at how to create a collaborate and cohesive assessment strategy.

A final stage in this planning process should be moderation where subject leaders and their teams can look at pedagogy, planned lessons and pupils' work and share a collective understanding about content, depth of learning and quality of output. Moderation, professional learning conversations and opportunities to share pedagogical approaches are all sustainable and cost-effective strategies for continuing professional development (CPD) and, combined with subject-specific and curriculum CPD, should lead to reassurances for those who lead in the primary phase that their curriculum ambition and rationale are building parity, high-quality outcomes and deep learning for staff and pupils across the school.

Conclusion

There is no doubt that the key to success in designing a curriculum that will deliver high-quality education outcomes for all pupils is in creating a powerful consensus. This coalition involves not just the senior leadership team but also those who have the responsibility for deciding the content and how it will be taught. Distributed leadership is, therefore, an essential element of any strategic planning (Rees, 2020).

The curriculum rationale must be communicated with clarity. There has to be a tacit understanding of the resource implications that high-quality curriculum design will require. This includes the essential need to ensure all subject leads have an opportunity to strengthen their expertise and understand the depth of knowledge their pupils should be exposed to. They also need to know the skills pupils need to access and make sense of their growing knowledge. There must be a consensus to look closely at the subject and cross-curricular concepts that knit the subject together and give pupils an opportunity to make connections across all their learning.

Creating the right strategy that builds consensus requires a commitment to providing the time, the CPD and the space for planning to take place. Subject-specific and cross-curricular dialogue will lead to a consensus that will identify how to build on prior learning, how to sequence the learning and how through the development of a progressive curriculum model it is clear that pupils are seamlessly moving towards carefully defined end points in their learning.

Top tips

- Take account of the experiences and learning that came from the need to work remotely and build a consensus that technology can play a part in creating opportunities for achieving high-quality curriculum outcomes
- Identify and celebrate the strengths and talents of all members of staff in the school
- Know the local context within which your school exists and how pupils can start here and then widen their experiences culturally and aesthetically
- Take account of the curriculum design concepts when planning the curriculum rationale and intent
- Reflect on the statement of curriculum intent and ensure that it is transparent and can be interpreted by all those who will deliver a deep, broad and balanced learning experience
- Focus on the domain-specific nature of educational leaders. Ensure a deep knowledge of the qualities of outstanding pedagogy and learning and how effective assessment strategies lead to progression and deep learning
- Have a deep focus on ensuring that all pupils have access to the same rich curriculum offer and that there is parity for all pupils within the school
- Have a good understanding of the aims within the National Curriculum programmes of study for each subject taught in school and how some of the concepts transcend subject-specific domains
- Insist that there is an emphasis in all subjects on creating opportunities for pupils to read widely and use mathematical skills where they apply in the context of subjects other than mathematics
- Create opportunities for cross-phase and cross-curricular planning time where teams can work together to develop sequential learning pathways that weave skills and knowledge together

References

Burns, R. (2020) 'Leading the primary curriculum: Developing subject leadership and expertise' *Impact* (9). Available at: https://my.chartered.college/impact_article/leading-the-primary-curriculum-developing-subject-leadership-and-expertise/ (accessed 27 July 2022).

Counsell, C. (2018) 'Senior Curriculum Leadership 1: The indirect manifestation of knowledge: (B) final performance as deceiver and guide', *The dignity of the thing*, 12 April 2018 [Blog]. Available at: https://thedignityofthethingblog.wordpress.com/2018/04/12/senior-curriculum-leadership-1-the-indirect-manifestation-of-knowledge-b-final-performance-as-deceiver-and-guide/ (accessed 27 July 2022).

Department for Education (DfE) (2014) *National Curriculum in England: Framework for Key Stages 1 and 2*. London: DfE.

Hargreaves, A. and O'Conner, M. T. (2018) *Collaborative Professionalism: When Teaching Together Means Learning for All*. Thousand Oaks, CA: Corwin Press.

Teaching Schools Council. Led by Keeble, R. (2016) *Review of Effective Primary Teaching Practice*, London.

Ofsted (2018) *The First Phase of Research into Curriculum Design*. London: Ofsted.

Ofsted (2019) *The Education Inspection Framework 2022 – Further Amendments Likely*. London: Ofsted.

Priestley, M. and Xenofontos, C. (2021) 'Curriculum making: key concepts and practices'. In Biddulph, J. and Flutter, J. (eds) *Inspiring Primary Curriculum Design. Unlocking Research*. Abingdon: Routledge.

Rees, T. (2020) A New Perspective for School Leadership, *Ambition Institute Blog*. Available at: https://www.ambition.org.uk/blog/2020-new-perspective-school-leadership/ (accessed 27 July 2022).

3

CREATING A HIGH-QUALITY CURRICULUM AS A TAPESTRY OF LEARNING: SKILLS, CONCEPTS AND KNOWLEDGE

The trick is to design a curriculum that helps children to acquire the knowledge in order to learn ever more complex skills, and then gives them opportunities to practice and apply them over time, in order to master them. This includes regular knowledge retrieval and application and revisiting and refining skills. An outstanding curriculum is one that is designed with these sequenced opportunities built into the progression model. (Cornerstones Education, 2020)

Creating a collaborative culture in pursuit of high-quality learning and teaching

Learning is a process that requires a coalition of minds. The curriculum is the map that defines the journey that pupils will take from their first day in reception to their last day in Year 6. A map is a representation of something much bigger and more complex but creates for the interpreter an opportunity to decipher the symbols and signs that lead to a clearly defined strategy of how to arrive on time without getting lost or deviating too far from the original plan. Senior leaders and their curriculum teams need to draw that map and carefully construct a suitable journey planner that everyone can follow.

Senior, subject and curriculum leaders need to build and cascade a schematic plan that focuses on how the curriculum develops to ensure depth and breadth and a sequencing of knowledge from Early Years to Year 6 and beyond.

The schema that will unfold as the map of curriculum intent must define the component parts that have been decided upon. These must include decisions about whether the approach to curriculum delivery is skills-led, knowledge-engaged or knowledge-led. The vision needs to tell how pupils will access knowledge, deepen that knowledge and be ready for the next stage of their education.

The components of a well-defined, deep and broad curriculum offer create the structure that builds on prior learning and allows for the deepening of knowledge acquisition (Brown et al., 2014). Where pupils have a bank of knowledge, new knowledge can be integrated more easily. Essentially, this building of a knowledge repository for the pupil will allow them to continue to add new knowledge to existing knowledge. The key is to ensure that all staff involved in the delivery of the curriculum to pupils build their own pedagogical repertoire that means pupils know what they are learning and can see how new knowledge is adding to their current understanding. For this they also need to be able to access the knowledge through the acquisition and continued practice of a range of increasingly complex skills.

This requires a collaboration and meeting of minds, time and strategic planning space for phase leaders and teachers, subject leaders and their teams and others involved such as teaching assistants to work together to create this multi-layered process (Howard and Hill, 2020).

As a starting point it is essential to break down the concepts that are essential for curriculum planning and ensure that it is clear to all those involved what each stage entails in terms of connecting knowledge, skills and cross-curricular themes to create a sequential curriculum offer that ensures all pupils learn deeply, make progress and are ready at the end of each year and key stage for the next phase of their education.

Explicitly defining the connection of knowledge to learning – Early Years to Year 6 and beyond

There is a strange contradiction when one delves deeply into the commentary about how the curriculum should be planned and delivered in relation to knowledge. The recent political point of view is that all in education should put the value of knowledge at the very heart of planning what will be taught (Policy Exchange, 2015). Knowledge is the outcome that every teacher and everyone responsible for the smooth running of a school is looking for pupils to have as they move on to the next stage of their education.

However, knowledge is the passive product of many other factors involved in the process of learning. Where the knowledge-led curriculum design approach is favoured there is always a tacit acknowledgement, for instance, that pupils must access that knowledge, make sense of it and use it to apply to other aspects of learning, make connections where knowledge transcends subjects and build deeper meaning over time. Knowledge is, therefore, a luxury for many learners who have yet to master the basic literacy, numeracy and thinking skills that are essential to absorb knowledge.

To focus on knowledge as the key to success for all learners is to forget that each one of them has started from a very different place. Some come from homes stuffed with books where their parents talk and share their ideas, passions and beliefs; others from homes where there are no books and parents do not have the skills, language or time to talk to their children. There are situations where pupils do not have the same level of vocabulary, confidence and oracy skills as others. Whatever their starting point there is a fundamental and essential need to make sure all pupils can read, use the spoken word fluently and write fluidly. Once these basic skills are mastered then accessing a wide body of knowledge becomes a possibility.

The Department for Education published a paper in July 2021 called *The Reading Framework – Teaching the Foundations of Literacy* which focuses on the absolute importance of reading as the fundamental skill all pupils need to have to be successful learners. The content focuses on more than just reading; it examines the value of oracy as an essential prerequisite to learning how to read showing that the wider a child's vocabulary in the pre-reading phase the more successful they are likely to be as readers. It also examines the importance of early use of phonics as the basis for learning how to read and it discusses the transition from reading to writing as an essential next step on the road to successful learning.

There is little in the Reading Framework that focuses on knowledge acquisition. Its absence confirms to me that in the Early Years and Key Stage 1 where most pupils will acquire the skills to use sounds to recognise words and begin to build their store of vocabulary and start learning how to read and then to write are the essential pre-cursers to accessing knowledge. This is not to say that learning to read does not also expose pupils to a body of knowledge, of course, it does. The priority for those planning and delivering the curriculum in these phases, however, is on the skills pupils must learn to even begin to absorb a wide body of knowledge. Therefore, in this phase the curriculum is undoubtedly skills-led. Within the DfE publication there are some excellent ideas, examples and resources to support those who have the role of helping pupils towards being proficient readers and there are several appendices that will be invaluable for all teachers, especially those who are relatively new to the profession.

> Without doubt, schools need to have a strong relationship with knowledge, particularly around what they want their pupils to know and know how to do. However, school leaders should recognise and understand that this does not mean that the curriculum should be formed from isolated chunks of knowledge, identified as necessary for passing a test.
>
> A rich web of knowledge is what provides the capacity for pupils to learn even more and develop their understanding. This does not preclude the importance of skill. Knowledge and skill are intrinsically linked: skill is a performance built on what a person knows.
>
> (Amanda Spielman, Ofsted Chief Inspector of Schools (2018) speaking at Conference of the Association for Science Educators)

Early Years and Key Stage 1 – essential core skills for learning

The Early Years Foundation Stage is a critical stage of learning. The role of the Early Years setting and the infant school is to create the environment for learning that ensures all pupils acquire the literacy and numeracy skills they will need to navigate the next stage of their learning journey. The pedagogy that is critical to this phase must also provide for pupils to learn wider thinking skills essential to their future potential. These include simple problem-solving, socialising through paired and group work, sharing, decision-making, interpreting and representing visual images and reasoning. The wealth of opportunity to acquire these skills through highly effective schema, planning to use different pedagogical approaches and strategies for reflection and reinforcement will build the knowledge and conceptual understanding as well as creating opportunities for pupils to become unconsciously competent in a range of core and wider skills.

The curriculum is a resource for charting the teacher's, the school's and a country's goals – what is valued that it is important that all pupils have access to. In contrast, pedagogy refers to how the teacher engages with the prior experiences of pupils and enables them to have access to the concepts of the curriculum. Through their involvement in pedagogy as learners, pupils come to see their experience in new ways; this may involve reading a poem or doing a chemistry experiment – the teacher's goal has always to be that the student has grasped the idea or the concept and can use it in any appropriate new context.

(Michael Young, Institute of Education, 2014)

The Key Stage 2 curriculum – sequencing a tapestry of skills and knowledge

A sound grounding in the core literacy and numeracy skills provides the springboard for learning in Key Stage 2 and creates the potential sequence of learning that will be the foundation for study at Key Stage 3 and beyond. In this phase it is my conviction that the most successful approach will be a knowledge-engaged process (Ofsted phase 1 research, 2018) where the skills are still a fundamental part of the decisions made about what should be taught and where careful consideration is given to how pupils will use a wide range of skills across all the foundation subjects to allow sequenced knowledge to be retained in the long-term memory.

Depth and breadth are important key concepts of curriculum design. The imperative to ensure that the curriculum offers pupils the opportunity to study a range of subjects in some detail linked to the National Curriculum creates for those with responsibility for implementing the curriculum intent with some complex responsibilities. Questions that need careful thought are:

- How does planning for lower Key Stage 2 and then in sequence upper Key Stage 2 take account of what was taught and learnt in EYFS and Key Stage 1?
- How does the planned curriculum allow pupils to access a range of specific subject knowledge?
- How will what is taught provide pupils with the opportunity to continue to develop expertise in deeper reading and comprehension, extended writing, speaking, presentation and listening skills, and a range of progressive numeracy skills that lead to mathematical fluency?
- What is the strategy for professional development to ensure all those who teach this phase have the knowledge, expertise and practical skill to deliver expert subject content?
- How is progression and sequencing of learning planned for every subject and where are the clear cross-curricular connections?
- How is assessment designed to shape future learning?
- What are the assessment strategies to show that the planned curriculum content and what pupils produce allows pupils to deepen and retain their understanding over time?

The curriculum in Key Stage 2 will be enriched by ensuring all teachers involved in planning and teaching have carefully considered essential components that will enhance their teaching. They must also create for pupils an experience that will ensure they understand what they are learning as well as identifying the skills they are using to access increasingly complex concepts and deep knowledge over time that will ultimately remain in the long-term memory. These components include building on prior learning and the sequencing of content and skills that demonstrate that pupils are progressing and acquiring powerful knowledge that they retain and can use to make connections across other subjects and topics they will encounter.

A further consideration and essential component is to almost start with what the school wants pupils to achieve by the end of Year 6. If this is articulated as the defined goal, then teachers can work together to decide the curriculum sequence from Early Years to Year 6. Even more profound is creating opportunities for curriculum leaders to liaise directly with their secondary school partners to look closely at what schools want pupils to know and be able to do so that they are ready at the beginning of Year 7 to fully access the Key Stage 3 curriculum.

There is a complex weaving of a variety of very important threads that need to be in place to show evidence that there is in fact a clear sequence to the learning and that includes some important elements contained in Table 3.1.

Table 3.1 The threads that bind the learning

Curriculum threads	Explanation
Subject specific vocabulary	Creating opportunities for teachers to identify the key words that are specific to the topic or series of lessons and that may be new to pupils ensures that the teaching can help pupils to comprehend these words, make sense of them in a particular context and maybe see where a similar word is familiar to them in a different subject context.
Cross-curricular concepts	Opportunities to look beyond the subject specific and create discussions about where specific concepts transcend subjects such as power, space, scale, conflict, equality, proportion etc. can reinforce understanding and deepen knowledge. Where such concepts are left unexplored the potential for deep learning is lost.
Mathematical fluency	There is within the quality framework that Ofsted have defined an imperative to ensure that the teaching of concepts in mathematics is translated into subject specific contexts across the curriculum. Learning fractions for instance can be reinforced by using fractions to create a pie chart that will be a visual representation of the population of cities in a country being studied in geography. Learning about shapes and angles can be reinforced in a design & technology lesson where pupils are making models such as boxes, picture frames or bird tables.
Comprehension and other literacy skills	All teaching and support staff are teachers of reading and are responsible for ensuring their pupils can comprehend what they read. It is therefore essential that pupils have access to a wide range of fiction and non-fiction texts that build their vocabulary, deepen their knowledge and create a thirst for knowledge and a love of reading. Other literacy skills learnt over time provide pupils with the tools to express, debate, explain, analyse, reflect and review.
Cultural Capital (SMSC)	Weaving an entitlement to opportunities for social, moral, spiritual and cultural experiences is motivating, exciting and leads to profound opportunities to reinforce the learning in the classroom. Planning the curriculum should include as many opportunities as possible, both virtually and physically for pupils to experience culture in their local context and where possible further afield.

The curriculum threads that are described in Table 3.1 are relevant across all of the subjects taught as part of the National Curriculum, both the core and the foundation subjects. Subject-specific content needs to be planned carefully in relation to the local and wider context within which the school exists. Explicit reference to the threads that bind the learning as described here will provide for subject leaders and their teams the opportunity to focus on the complexities and cross-curricular connections that create the evidence that there is a synergy between the planning and delivery of a deep and rich curriculum offer.

None of the above are subject-specific and provide for curriculum leaders and their teams opportunities to find the links that will help pupils to make vital connections across a range of subjects. There are many possibilities to create a rich tapestry that will enhance the learning and build for the pupil a deeper understanding of how they can use their skills and growing knowledge to make sense of a range of different subjects. Cognitive science suggests that it is these kinds of relationships that will support pupils to take in knowledge that through reinforcement and correlation will lead to the learning entering and remaining in the long-term memory.

Observing, learning, refining pedagogy and building the language of the 'deep dive'

Figure 3.1 illustrates the three component parts of the research undertaken by Ofsted in June 2019. The first segment relates to the emphasis on importance placed on lesson observation and focuses on how teachers interpret the curriculum intent and then translate it into high-quality pedagogy and learning. The lower segment is about putting the spotlight on what is being produced by pupils as a result of their learning. The third element, is the emphasis on the need to make sure there is a collaborative approach to ensuring the curriculum is sequenced, is seamless and delivers the highest quality learning experience for all pupils and their teachers.

As discussed in Chapter 1, Ofsted's research from the summer of 2019 focuses on a triangulation model for how to evaluate the quality of education in relation to the curriculum and how it is taught and assessed.

It is, as a result of this research, that Ofsted began to talk about their 'deep dive' strategy. Creating a culture where there is a collaborative approach to defining what quality means in relation to education requires individuals and teams to share their ideas, decisions and areas of concern. The potential to add conversations not just with

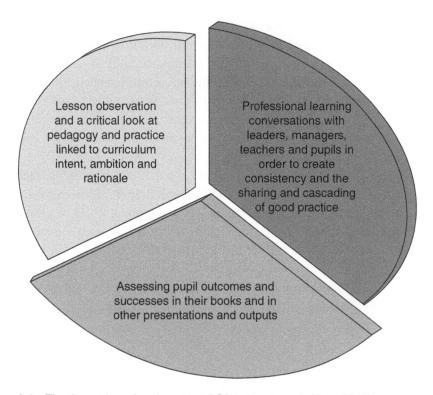

Figure 3.1 The three triangular elements of Ofsted's research (June 2019)

the headteacher but also with subject experts, teachers, teaching assistants and pupils provides a balanced and more accurate view of how the school is performing. A lesson observation snapshot or outputs from books and other media will go so far but a deeper more informed view comes through adding the qualitative to the quantitative and making a judgement that embraces both.

We have so far looked at the complex web of skills, content and concepts that are within and transcend all the subjects the curriculum embraces. Ofsted have provided some interesting guidance for schools to use to navigate and arrive safely at a collaborative and creative curriculum offer that will deliver high-quality learning. It does not on first reading look as if it is specific to schools. It is, in fact, written to test the validity of the inspection process. It was formulated as a triangulation that included an in-depth look at lesson observation, a focus on what pupils produce and therefore how they are assessed and the third element, how the use of professional conversations provides the glue that knits together the qualitative and quantitative and demonstrates that there is indeed cohesion in how the curriculum is planned and delivered.

> Conversations with leaders, teachers and pupils can provide the vital context we need to understand what we see. These conversations are central to the deep dive model.

However, relying purely on what people tell us would be problematic in an inspection context. This is why we need first-hand evidence from pupils' work and lesson visits among other sources, such as attainment in national tests.

(Research commentary: Assessing the quality of education (Ofsted, July 2019), Sean Harford blog (2019))

The three strands of research undertaken by Ofsted between 2017 and 2019 informed the content of their Inspection Handbook for Schools, first published in September 2019. There have been several revisions since then, particularly in relation to school priorities that became pressing as a result of the pandemic and school closures. Now post-pandemic, a revised handbook for September 2022 sends a clear message that schools must pick up the baton in relation to coherence as to the curriculum, 'what is taught and why and how topics are sequenced and schemas built' (Spielman, 2022).

Amanda Spielman also emphasised her belief in the power of the professional conversation in her speech at the Festival of Education at Westminster College in July 2022:

I've spoken a great deal about the power of professional dialogue between school leaders and inspectors. That dialogue should be the engine room – sparking ideas and helping shape the school's next steps.

(Amanda Spielman, July 2022)

Looking in detail at the first element of the triangulation, lesson observation provides a list of indicators used in the original research. It is broken down into three key indicators:

- Curriculum
- Teaching
- Behaviour

The indicators for lesson observation which are listed in Chapter 1 are interested in the skills as much as the knowledge of and focus on equality of opportunity, challenge, sequencing, recall and practice, and relevant and clear assessment.

These provide school leaders and others who engage in measuring quality assurance of the curriculum with a focus on key elements of curriculum implementation and how well individual teachers are delivering a curriculum that matches the stated aims and rationale, and the intent.

The following questions might help subject leaders to work closely with their teams to share a dialogue as to what might create high-quality lessons and what should be a focus in relation to what is being taught (the knowledge), how teachers support pupils towards depth of understanding and competence (the pedagogy) and how teachers know that their planning, teaching and schema are having an impact on learning for all pupils (assessment).

- How does the lesson demonstrate that the teacher has the relevant subject expertise?
- How does the observer assess that all pupils have the same access to curriculum content?
- What is the evidence that shows how teachers support pupils who need help with basic literacy and numeracy?
- What is meant by 'suitably demanding' and 'appropriate lesson content'?
- How do teachers show inspectors that the lesson he or she is observing is part of a 'logical sequence' of learning?
- What are the pedagogical strategies that teachers are using to demonstrate that they are providing opportunities for pupils to recall and practise previously learned skills and knowledge?
- How is assessment providing information that shines a window on the current skills and knowledge of pupils?

The second set of indicators focus specifically on the teaching in relation to the qualities a teacher possesses that allow learning to take place. So, the skills indicated here are:

- Effective communication skills
- Clear use of presentation that builds knowledge and allows pupils to make connections
- The use of relevant and appropriate resources
- Incisive questioning skills
- The ability to give explicit, detailed and constructive feedback
- There is evidence that teachers accurately check for understanding

These indicators offer a rich vein of opportunity for the development of highly effective professional conversations. Subject leaders and their teams can share their understanding of how the indicators translate into good-quality classroom practice and provide the opportunity to begin to articulate how the curriculum is delivering quality outcomes that ensure success for both the pupil and their teacher.

- How do you quantify good communication skills?
- What is the impact of effective communication skills on the pupil's capacity to learn?
- How accessible and clear are presentations used by teachers and how are they used to challenge pupils to build knowledge and make connections?
- How relevant and accessible are the resources used in lessons so that their use deepens the pupils' knowledge and understanding?
- How do teachers know that pupils can comprehend and understand the resources they read and use?
- What evidence is there that questioning by the teachers creates the autonomy and motivation that pupils need to find their own solutions, innovate and take risks with their learning?
- How does assessment lead to learning?

The challenge is to create professional learning communities within school or across a group of schools. This will ensure that the expertise that will be strong within many subject areas can be shared so that informal CPD helps to create powerful answers to the questions. This gives each teacher the answers to a whole range of possibilities in more than one context. This will help to build their confidence and allow them to own their own deep understanding of what really does constitute a high-quality curriculum offer. There is a more detailed look at professional learning communities in Chapter 8.

Continuity in assessing the learning

We now need to focus on the last segment of the triangle, the focus on what pupils are producing and how the work is assessed so that all those involved can assess the learning, recognise misconceptions, identify gaps in learning and where pupils need to be stretched and challenged.

Ofsted created a grid shown in Table 3.2 to explain their indicators for 'book' scrutiny (Ofsted, 2019).

Although the focus of Ofsted's research is on 'book' scrutiny, these indicators can apply more broadly to many of the other elements of output produced by pupils. Some of their best work will be in situations far more exciting and creative than written work in their books. The rule of thumb is to celebrate all of the possibilities to showcase the incredible work that pupils across all schools produce and put it in the way of anyone who wants to dive deeply into what is possible.

Table 3.2 Evidence of progression through the evaluation of what pupils produce and create

Building on previous learning	Depth and breadth of coverage	Pupil progress	Practice
Pupils' knowledge is consistently, coherently and logically sequenced so that it can develop incrementally over time. There is a progression from the simpler and/or more concrete concepts to the more complex and/or abstract ones. Pupils' work shows that they have developed their knowledge and skills over time.	The content of the tasks and pupils' work show that pupils learn a suitably broad range of topics within a subject. Tasks also allow pupils to deepen their knowledge of the subject by requiring thought on their part, understanding of subject-specific concepts and making connections to prior knowledge.	Pupils make strong progress from their starting points. They acquire knowledge and understanding appropriate to their starting points.	Pupils are regularly given opportunities to revisit and practice what they know to deepen and solidify their understanding in a discipline. They can recall information effectively, which shows that learning is durable. Any misconceptions are addressed and there is evidence to show that pupils have overcome these in future work.

Explaining the science that links knowledge, memory and deep learning

Learning ... that reflective activity which enables the learner to draw upon previous experience to understand and evaluate the present, so as to shape future action and formulate knowledge.

(NSIN Research Matters, quoting Abbott, 1994)

Essentially, cognitive science explains how pupils learn and provides an insight into what prevents some pupils from progressing well. Throughout this chapter the exploration has been into the component contents of a well-constructed and sequenced curriculum that delivers pupils who are equipped with the skills and knowledge for the next stage of their education. We have also explored the elements of pedagogy or teaching that an inspector might look for when observing learning in the classroom. The reasons why some of these approaches work is in the realm of academic theoretical science.

There is currently a recommendation for Ofsted that all teachers should have training in the basics of cognitive science linked to their role in the classroom. There is little space for this in many current initial teacher training programmes and for experienced teachers already qualified and well into their teaching career this maybe is something they feel is not relevant to their own day-to-day practice.

However, the broad principles that underpin this branch of science are reassuringly familiar to all those who teach or who teach teachers how to teach. Research into cognitive science is wide and well documented. A recent piece of research by the Education Endowment Foundation (2021) looks at how the research is put into practice in classrooms. It provides a comprehensive look at the science and is practical, accessible and well-structured. There are many other places to go to find out more about the role of cognitive science on memory, behaviour and creating the right conditions for learning.

The key principles that those involved in planning the curriculum can focus on without delving into a deep academic study of this complex science are:

- Learning requires information to be committed to the long term-memory
- Information is processed through the working memory
- The working memory has limited capacity and can become overloaded

Understanding these three key principles Kolb (1990) then provides the curriculum planner and the teacher with decisions to make about how to teach specific literacy and numeracy skills to young learners, how to introduce new subject knowledge to pupils beginning to learn through geography or understanding characters and the plot in an English context. In order for pupils to learn, the teacher must help pupils to use their working memory, to take in information and to use it as part of learning facts or embarking on specific tasks. Pupils learn best when they are motivated, interested and engaged and therefore choose to listen, concentrate or follow instructions given in order that they can benefit from using their working memory. Weak working memory skills can affect learning in all subject areas. Where pupils have the opportunity to see certain concepts across a range of subject this will stimulate their working memory (Sealy, 2020).

Cognitive load theory examines how easy it is for the working memory to become overloaded and lead to no learning taking place. It is, therefore, essential that teachers understand the importance of this theory and how best to stimulate a pupil's ability to remember what they are learning and not feel overwhelmed.

Creating the right conditions that ensure cognitive load is avoided, teachers need to think about how they remove all unnecessary information (intrinsic load) and avoid distractions such as excessive noise, an overly busy classroom and too much information at once (extraneous load) so that the essential information and knowledge is highlighted and retained by pupils (germane load).

The aim, of course, is to stimulate the working memory so that the learning is then translated into the long-term memory where it will stay. In order to do this the teacher must create the right atmosphere where all pupils pay attention to the learning in order to absorb the knowledge into their working memory. It is here that a series of strategies can take shape to support the pupil to learn deeply so that the information or knowledge moves from the working to the long-term memory. Pupils need opportunities to rehearse, repeat and retrieve information so that they do not forget what is in their working memory or lose it due to cognitive overload (Williams, 2014).

Planning the right pedagogy linked to an understanding of how pupils learn, retrieve and retain knowledge is the key to creating the evidence that pupils are learning and building a body of knowledge that deepens over time and that allows them to make connections, reason, problem solve and be ready to undertake increasingly challenging and difficult tasks or activities.

Some examples of how teachers can support pupils to retain and retrieve knowledge so that it moves from the working memory to the long-term memory are:

- **Dual-coding** – enhancing the learning through the use of pictorial or other visual and graphical images. This can also be coupled with multimedia learning where technology is introduced to support the enhancement of knowledge acquisition
- **Spaced learning** – Distributing learning and retrieval opportunities over a longer period of time rather than concentrating them altogether within one single topic. The spaces can be filled with unrelated content where the pupil is likely to forget and can then be encouraged to recall and remember thus strengthening the learning and helping it to remain in the long-term memory
- **Interleaving** is similar to spaced learning but the content of what fills the spaces in the learning is similar and connected

- **Retrieval practice** – Providing opportunities for pupils to recall information using many different approaches such as multiple-choice quizzes, the use of flash cards, practice tests, or fish diagrams and mind-mapping
- **Managing cognitive load** – creating the right conditions for pupils to listen, take in relevant information and not be distracted by unnecessary content, unhelpful graphics, pictures or diagrams or given material that is irrelevant or superfluous
- **Working with schemas** – a schema is a framework or concept that helps the pupil or the teacher to organise and interpret information. The use of knowledge organisers or mind-maps can help with conceptual learning as can using diagrams. Schemas can help to scaffold the learning and can have a positive impact on the cognitive lead because the information is compartmentalised for the pupil

The broad principles within the study of cognitive science that might influence thinking in the context of planning to ensure deep learning and knowledge acquisition are listed below:

- Small incremental steps support the acquisition of detailed knowledge over time
- A focus on culture in a local and then a wider context to stimulate pupils' interests
- Creating opportunities for pupils to make connections within and across subjects
- Carefully sequencing the knowledge over time so that pupils retain their learning
- Emphasising the difference between the subject disciplines creates the context for decisions about what to teach and when

The interplay between cognitive science and practical approaches to teacher development

There is a lot of interest in cognitive science theory and its impact on the quality of education specifically linked to teaching and learning. However, its application relies on a number of important factors and unless carefully constructed as a method of developing outstanding pedagogy it may impede progress. Consideration needs to made as to where and how these techniques are included in professional development activity. For new teachers learning their craft, classroom practice is critical and where these techniques are taught they need to be practised in the classroom and reflected upon through the use of excellent feedback techniques. Being aware of cognitive science theory can improve pedagogical practice but may not do so if the theory replaces reflective practice in the classroom. It would be a bit like asking someone to read a book about how to drive a car and then expect them to be fully competent behind the wheel.

Teachers must have a profound understanding of how pupils learn, therefore an understanding of the cognitive science that defines learning is important. The way teachers were trained in the first place will provide some indication of their prior knowledge in relation to cognitive science. If they know it they may well be a little reluctant to be faced with the theory when they already know its impact in the classroom. However, revisiting some of the theory may be useful, especially where it impacts on pupil motivation, memory capacity, attention span and well-being issues. The link between nutrition and hydration and concentration are worth comment as are the whole issue of attention following months of home schooling and loss of self-esteem and confidence. Some of the theories and approaches discussed must be planned in relation to the age, personality, ability and interests of the pupil.

There is also a need to focus on the pupils and their environment and how these approaches support them in how well they learn, for example the pupils and their own culture and family setting, attention to the classroom environment so that it is not too busy, too noisy, too bright or too cold. Time to focus on the walls and their 'busy-ness' and what is available for pupils to use in terms of materials and resources especially books and other reading material.

Lastly, there is an imperative to focus on the knowledge and how it is taught as part of subject-specific content or in relation to a more concept-based cross-curricular approach. Some of the techniques or pedagogies such as interleaving, spacing and scaffolding all support the development of knowledge through the acknowledgement that learning across a range of concepts can in fact enhance the ability of the pupil to remember over a longer period of time and allow for pupils to access that knowledge to further deepen their understanding (Hirsch, 2002).

I include this final consideration for cognitive science as is currently in vogue. However, there are many ways to enhance the professional development opportunities for teachers and others in the profession. It is experience, opportunities for reflection and the sharing of good and outstanding practice that will ultimately help all those who teach to improve and grow in their role. The cognitive science is implicit and for many it is best left that way.

Conclusion

Those with senior leadership responsibility need to make decisions about the curriculum that define what will be taught, how it will be taught and how the work that pupils produce will be assessed. An understanding of the recent research into curriculum design should give curriculum planners the relevant evidence that will inform their choices as to the approach they need to take. The emphasis on knowledge needs careful consideration, especially for very young children who must learn the basic skills before they are able to access powerful knowledge.

As pupils move into Key Stage 2 skills remain a critical and essential element of the learning, especially a deep focus on reading and literacy and number and deeper maths skills. The opportunities to reinforce literacy, whether it is reading, writing, listening or speaking are indisputably there in every subject. The opportunity to explicitly build on learning in English across a range of other subjects will help pupils to make connections and create opportunities for them to become confident and skilful in their use of the English language. Equally, it is palpably a missed opportunity not to make explicit where maths skills are an integral part of learning across a range of foundation subjects. Pupils will benefit greatly from understanding how the concepts they learn in maths lessons apply in context elsewhere in the curriculum.

The application of cognitive science as the key to understanding how pupils learn is important and teachers should have a theoretical understanding of the principles that underpin the sequencing of learning where pupils absorb information into their short-term memory and then through retrieval practice, recall and reinforcement will eventually retain the knowledge in their long-term memory and can access it for many other applications.

The curriculum indicators for good curriculum design are clearly defined in recent research and suggest that high-quality educational outcomes include that the curriculum builds on prior learning and sequences the learning over time so that pupils arrive at clearly defined end points ready for the next stage of their education. A combination of both implicit and explicit conversations and CPD that explain the theory and opportunities to share and celebrate good and best practice in both subject-specific and cross-curricular contexts will create the professional conversations that will provide the evidence and a collaborative dialogue for any number of 'deep dive' questions from whoever chooses to ask them.

Top tips

- Make sure intent defines how the curriculum will be taught and quantifies how knowledge will be accessed and successfully learnt over time
- Create the opportunity for subject leaders to work with their colleagues from across the curriculum to look at a range of programmes of study that connect knowledge, skills and cross-curricular themes and that will build a sequential curriculum
- Ensure reading is a priority in all lessons, across all subjects and in cross- and extra-curricular activities
- A priority in EYFS and Key Stage 1 must be to ensure all pupils have the basic literacy and numeracy skills as essential building blocks of learning
- All those with responsibility for planning and delivering the curriculum at Key Stage 1 and 2 need to understand and be able to consistently articulate how the school is focusing on building on prior knowledge and learning, the sequencing of the content and how pupils are making connections across their learning
- Plan backwards, taking account of the ambition your school has for all its learners when they move to the next stage of their education
- Create opportunities in meetings, CPD sessions and within departments and teams for collaborative professional conversations to take place about the

curriculum and how intent is translating into implementation so that there is a consistent message
- Where subject leaders and their teams do not have the relevant subject expertise ensure explicit opportunities exist for immersive CPD to build their capacity to teach the subject
- Focus on to what extent cognitive science and its value in creating a deeper understanding of how pupils learn should be an essential part of the CPD offer. Audit who needs this the most
- Look closely through lesson observation and in other opportunities to focus on learning in the classroom and evaluate the potential for learning, the acquisition of knowledge and potential cognitive overload

References

Abbot, J. (1994) *Learning Makes Sense: Re-creating Education for a Changing Future*. Letchworth: Education 2000.

Brown, P., Roediger, H. and McDaniel, M. (2014) *Make It Stick*. Cambridge, MA: Harvard University Press.

Cornerstones (2020) *Cornerstones Curriculum*. South Yorkshire: Cornerstones.

Department for Education (DfE) (2021) *The Reading Framework: Teaching the Foundations of Literacy*. London: DfE.

Education Endowment Foundation (2021) *Cognitive Science Approaches in the Classroom*. London: Education Endowment Foundation.

Hirsch, E. D. (2016) *Why Knowledge Matters*. Cambridge, MA: Harvard University Press.

Howard, K. and Hill, C. (2020) *Symbiosis: The Curriculum and the Classroom*. Woodbridge: John Catt Educational.

Kolb, D. A. (1990) *Experiential Learning: Experience and the Source of Learning and Development*. Englewood Cliffs, NJ: Prentice Hall.

Spielman, A. (2018) *Ofsted Chief Inspector of Schools speaking at Conference of the Association for Science Educators*

Ofsted (2019) *Inspecting Education Quality: Lesson Observation and Workbook Scrutiny*. London: Ofsted.

Percival, A. (2020) 'Curriculum Building in the Primary School'. In Sealy, C. (ed.) *The researchED Guide to the Curriculum*. Woodbridge: John Catt Educational.

Policy Exchange (2015) *Knowledge and the Curriculum: A Collection of Essays to Accompany E. D. Hirsch's Lecture at the Policy Exchange*. London: Policy Exchange.

Sealy, C. (2020) 'Learning and Memory in the Classroom: What Teachers Should Know (Especially After the Summer)', *Third Space Learning Blog*, 6 June 2022 [Blog]. Available at: https://thirdspacelearning.com/blog/science-memory-forgetting-beat-summer-brain-drain-primary-school/ (accessed 27 July 2022).

Spielman, A. (2022) *Amanda Spielman's Speech to the Festival of Education, 2022.* [Speech transcript] Festival of Education, Wellington College, Crowthorne. 8 July 2022. Available at: https://www.gov.uk/government/speeches/amanda-spielmans-speech-to-the-festival-of-education-2022 (accessed 27 July 2022).

Williams, J. C. (2013) *Towards a Standards Based Curriculum: A Toolkit for the New Primary Curriculum in England.* London: Publish Nation.

4

SKILLS FOR LEARNING: WEAVING LITERACY, NUMERACY AND THINKING SKILLS ACROSS THE CURRICULUM

The aim of our curriculum is to prepare our pupils, ensuring they are equipped with the full range of skills that allows them to be lifelong learners ready for the next steps in their education and as well as preparing them for the wider world.
(Abbotswood Primary School – part of their explanation of curriculum intent (2021))

Skills development: an essential part of planning the primary curriculum

Pupils begin their primary journey in early years and have up to eight years of schooling in preparation for the next stage in their education, the secondary school. Their ability and potential at this early stage in their development will depend very much on their home life, their place in the family and their exposure to language, cultural and sensory experiences and the opportunity to interact with their peers, adults and others in society. It is the job of the school – and specifically their teachers – to assess their level of ability and define the pedagogical approaches that will help pupils to learn, develop their potential and allow them to gain the confidence to accept new challenges. It is in the early years where independent, active and participative learning is most in evidence and it is to here where we should look carefully at the importance of skills development and how these skills are an essential ingredient of all learning, particularly in the primary phase.

Developing a range of essential skills is paramount to any curriculum plan for the Early Years Foundation Stage (EYFS). Pupils must learn to form letters, to hear them and to turn them into words. They must have access and be exposed to as many opportunities as possible to play with words, see them, hear them and pronounce them.

Number skills are also, unsurprisingly, a key feature of the EYFS curriculum – learning how to count and recognising numbers, shapes and symbols all create the building blocks for a future where the learning of mathematical concepts and how they shape our world can create wonder and a life-long love of the patterns and possibilities of numbers.

As pupils move from Early Years into Key Stage 1 and then 2, skills development continues to play an enormous part in the learning potential of every pupil. Recent thinking that knowledge is the starting point for planning for progression and a sequence to learning still means a focus on developing highly tuned comprehension skills and fluid handwriting and keyboard skills for demonstrating an increasing grasp of concepts, knowledge and information within all of the curriculum programmes of study. Acquiring numeracy skills is, of course, one of the essential core skills within the primary curriculum. The increasing depth of knowledge and understanding is underpinned by the need to continually practice and learn through rote and retrieval a suite of important development tools such as number bonds, times tables, the ability to use zero in a continuous way and the solving of simple mathematical problems (Williams, 2014).

Creating a curriculum map that looks across the full range of curriculum subjects and defines the skills as well as the knowledge that pupils will acquire on their journey towards Year 6 and beyond requires a collaboration of minds and cross-phase planning that plots the essential elements of learning from early years through Key Stage 1 and into Key Stage 2. An excellent starting point is to look at the rationale and ambition the school has documented in its vision or intent statement for pupils at the end of Key Stage 2 and to then work backwards to plot the sequence of learning in the core and foundation subjects within each year.

Deep learning that dovetails English and literacy with the wider foundation subjects

Many primary schools use the morning to teach English and maths and the afternoons to focus on the foundation subjects or on more topic-driven approaches that incorporate several of the foundation curriculum subject areas. This can fragment the drive to build high-quality core literacy and numeracy skills and lead to an emphasis on the task in hand rather than a real focus on enhancing skills competence and deepening the knowledge within a particular area of study. For instance, a topic on the Romans and their occupation of Britain may focus on Roman costume, Roman settlements and Roman architecture. It is easy within any one of these topics to be sidetracked into making costumes, building houses or looking at ruins so that it is the making of the model or object or the building or the trip itself that becomes the focus and not the development of the knowledge and the powerful opportunity to use discussion, creative writing, investigation or reading as the medium to find out more about the Romans and their time in Britain.

Building a Roman settlement should also incorporate powerful numeracy skills that focus on the shapes of the walls which are rectangles and the angles needed to put the rectangles together to make the walls safe and straight. Equally, a focus on the shape of a roof may reveal an apex, a triangle with angles, that ensure strength and accuracy in construction.

Similarly, a geography lesson where pupils are learning how to read a map has the potential for not to be missed opportunities for discussion, reading symbols and writing a journey planner or diary of an imaginary or real trip that the map would lead them towards. The numeracy skills are phenomenal and exciting – learning scale, for instance, can be a journey of discovery. Contour lines measure the percentage of a slope and creating opportunities to calculate how steep a hill is could lead to all sorts of discussion about the best route for walking or cycling.

There are so many opportunities to highlight numeracy and literacy skills that pupils are learning in their English and maths lessons across the foundation subjects. Raising awareness of how pupils are learning the concepts in their core learning and then applying that learning in the foundation subjects allows pupils to make real connections that will help them to remember their core learning in a more meaningful way which helps so much with cognitive ability over time.

Speaking and listening: essential prerequisites to learning, reasoning and progression

Children need to talk if they are to read well; they need to talk and read to stimulate thinking, and they need to think for themselves in order to write creatively and effectively. (Myatt, 2018)

Mary Myatt, in her book *The Curriculum: Gallimaufry to Coherence*, puts the case for taking speaking much more seriously with a distinct need to focus on ensuring pupils have the opportunity for high-quality talk. The fact that it is seen as the poor relation of the four skills of speaking, listening, reading and writing is not surprising as we as teachers continue to be judged on what our pupils produce in relation to the written word. Too much talk in the classroom might be seen as noisy, potentially a class out of control and a teacher not actually teaching.

It is my experience that creating opportunities for pupils to talk about their learning, share their ideas and exchange views on what they have read or make predictions about what comes next produce the best ever written work. Talk is an essential element of learning allowing pupils to come up with their own ideas, share their understanding or explain why they don't agree with the status quo. Creating the right conditions for pupils to talk is a powerful way to ensure that they write with deeper clarity and demonstrate their mastery of the knowledge they are discussing. Discussion, debate and presentation all reinforce understanding.

Ensuring pupils are exposed to a wide range of challenging and subject-specific vocabulary is an essential part of helping them to be ready to learn across the whole range of core and foundation subjects. However, they need to talk about the words, understand how certain words are pronounced, speak them in a context. The sooner pupils gain confidence in talking about the words they are learning in relation to the subject-specific knowledge they are asked to grasp the more likely they are to demonstrate how deeply they have understood in the context of their written work. Speaking allows pupils to savour the words, explore them and order them in a way that demonstrates that they have deepened their knowledge and understanding.

The National Curriculum does not define a sequential approach to speaking but provides a bulleted list of what should be achieved between Year 1 and Year 6. It is reproduced here:

Pupils should be taught to:

- Listen and respond appropriately to adults and their peers
- Ask relevant questions to extend their understanding and knowledge
- Use relevant strategies to build their vocabulary
- Articulate and justify answers, arguments and opinions
- Give well-structured descriptions, explanations and narratives for different purposes, including for expressing feelings
- Maintain attention and participate actively in collaborative conversations, staying on topic and initiating and responding to comments
- Use spoken language to develop understanding through speculating, hypothesising, imagining and exploring ideas
- Speak audibly and fluently with an increasing command of Standard English
- Participate in discussions, presentations, performances, role play, improvisations and debates
- Gain, maintain and monitor the interest of the listener(s)
- Consider and evaluate different viewpoints, attending to and building on the contributions of others
- Select and use appropriate registers for effective communication

(DfE programme of study for English Key Stage 1 and 2 (2014))

Teachers need time to focus on some of the opportunities for learning that the above list provides. For instance, 'Give well-structured descriptions, explanations and narratives for different purposes' needs time to plan for. What is a well-structured description? How can teachers develop the skills of pupils to begin to provide well-organised verbal presentations that demonstrate their knowledge and understanding. Where across the curriculum are there opportunities for pupils to create narratives of their own or provide a well-ordered presentation of a topic or issue, they have been learning about. Using the above list to create real opportunities for the development of effective speakers, presenters and storytellers over the whole of their primary school life is profound.

This area of the curriculum is not externally tested and does not require specific assessment but the opportunities to develop pupils' knowledge through oracy should not be missed. One of the important aspects of an inspection is that inspectors want to talk to pupils about their learning. The more pupils are given the time and the space to learn through their skills in oracy the more confidence they will gain; the more they can learn from each other and the more they can begin to question, infer, analyse, evaluate and justify, learning all the time in a fashion that deepens their knowledge and understanding. This should never be the reason for focusing on oracy but learners who articulate well will impress an inspection team.

Table 4.1 An all-embracing framework for speaking and listening 'The Oracy Framework' (Voice 21 and Oracy Cambridge, 2018)

Physical	Linguistic	Cognitive	Social and emotional
Voice Pace of speaking Tonal variation Pronunciation Voice projection **Body language** Gesture and posture Facial expression Eye contact	**Vocabulary** Register Grammar **Rhetorical techniques** Metaphor Humour Irony Mimicry	**Content** – Choice of content to convey meaning & intention – Building on the views of others **Structure** – Structure & organisation of talk **Clarifying & summarising** – Seeking information & clarification through questioning – Summarising **Reasoning** – Giving reasons to support views	**Paired and group working** Working with others **Active listening** Listening and responding **Confidence** Confidence in speaking **The audience** Audience awareness

Voice 21 have produced an oracy framework that unpicks the elements of oracy that are so important to learning (see Table 4.1).

The oracy framework as defined by Voice 21

The content of this framework provides the imaginative teacher with food for thought when planning how to include oracy or speaking and listening as part of the journey towards deep understanding of core or foundation learning within subjects or within themes and topics.

Focusing simply on talking and the spoken word is to forget the importance of listening as its sister and essential partner in the process of using oracy to good effect. To listen actively and well is a skill that escapes many of us. It is rarely taught explicitly and where adults are not very good at it, there is little chance that pupils in the classroom will be very good at it. Take time to specifically focus on the skill of listening as part of planned learning activities. It's pretty old-fashioned but still highly revealing to play Chinese Whispers or to quiz pupils about certain details in a passage that is read to them. These kinds of activities provide an opportunity to raise awareness of the importance of listening as a fundamental skill for learning and to actively teach it in the classroom.

Here are ten pieces of advice for raising the awareness of pupils as to the importance of them listening actively to their teacher, to their peers and to the various media that form a part of their learning.

- Concentrate on the person who is speaking, stop doing anything else except listening
- Think about how what you heard made you feel
- Look at the teacher and focus on any visual clues that are being used
- Talk about what you heard with a partner and share your thoughts about what was said
- You should not have to listen for long periods of time – think about what you will say when you have finished listening
- Write down what you have learnt and how by listening well you have understood
- Tell the teacher if you don't understand what you have heard
- Take notes using the key words and impressions from your listening
- Make pictures with what is being said, see the character, period in history or the object being talked about
- Draw what you have heard using a mind-map or symbols

There is good evidence that teachers are not good listeners when it comes to their pupils in the classroom and beyond. Learning how to listen actively is a profound skill for teachers working with their pupils, it is also an essential skill for managers and leaders to chair meetings, feedback on performance and support their teams with issues and problems that arise.

Here are some thoughts on how teachers can become more astute at listening to their pupils and hearing what they need, know and can do:

- Create the right atmosphere for listening
- Understand yourself, your voice, your body language
- Know all your pupils well and focus on their capacity for listening
- Talk less to ensure pupils can listen actively
- Give pupils time to discuss what they have heard with their peers
- Make pupils accountable for what they are listening to
- Give pupils time to write down or draw what they have heard
- Model good listening by listening accurately to pupils
- Encourage attentiveness – ask impromptu questions, ask for the key points
- Make sure what you are saying has structure and is easy to follow
- Vary tone, build suspense, emphasise or repeat the important bits
- Make sure pupils understand the value of listening as part of learning well

Reading, vocabulary, comprehension and the rich capacity for deep learning

Reading is a process of constructing meaning by interacting with text; as individuals read, they use their prior knowledge along with clues from the text to construct meaning. Research indicates that effective or expert readers are strategic (Baker and Brown, 1984a, 1984b). This means that they have purposes for their reading and adjust their reading to each purpose and for each reading task. Strategic readers use a variety of strategies and skills as they construct meaning.

(Paris et al., 1991)

In England the programmes of study for English at Key Stage 1 and 2 emphasise the need to look beyond the English lesson as part of creating for the pupil a wealth of opportunities to read deeply and widely.

The first four points in the aims section at the beginning of the programme of study are the same for Key Stage 1 and 2 and ask teachers to plan for pupils to:

- Read easily, fluently and with good understanding
- Develop the habit of reading widely and often, for both pleasure and information
- Acquire a wide vocabulary, an understanding of grammar and knowledge of linguistic conventions for reading, writing and spoken language
- Appreciate our rich and varied literary heritage

There is nothing in the text to suggest that the aims are purely for lessons in English, except for the title of the document. The opportunity to read easily, fluently and with good understanding is essential whatever the pupil is reading, be it a bus timetable, a recipe, a design specification, information about the Romans, books about aeroplanes. It is, however, incumbent on the teacher to make sure that the same level of care is taken as in an English lesson to make sure that pupils understand what they are reading, can make sense of the vocabulary and are fluent in how they read and interpret the text.

Reading is the key to successful learning. Where pupils access books and other printed material from an early age other than at school they become adept at reading much more quickly than where there is a dearth of reading material. This is out of the control of schools, but they can attempt to redress the balance for those where books are scarce at home by making sure that every classroom from Reception to Year 6 has a wealth of reading material for pupils to use as part of their learning.

There needs to be a symbiosis with the school library. Classroom teachers and library staff need to work together to make sure that books of a suitable reading age and subject matter are readily available along with advice for pupils as to what they should choose to read.

One of the simplest ways I have seen to fill up the classroom with a wealth of books on all sorts of subjects is to scour the local charity shops and buy whatever is there that is relevant and accessible to a particular year group or cohort. It doesn't matter how battered they become from a lot of use, they may even become a part of a project and be cut up to illustrate a topic or stress a point. There will be plenty more the next time you shop.

Reading for pleasure is also an essential element of becoming a fluent and happy reader. The content, the story, the suspense and the accessibility of the language will all create the atmosphere that will mean a pupil wants to pursue the story, find out more or learn new facts. The teacher needs to be vigilant and careful with their choices. A whole-class text may not suit every pupil so if these are used then the teacher needs to be able to justify to every pupil why this particular book is worth persevering with. There are many of us reading this paragraph who will remember their own experience of having to plough through a book for which they have no interest or cannot understand any of it.

The English language is rich and complicated and the sooner pupils become aware of its many quirks and anomalies the more likely they are to master its complexity. One of the memories that will live with me always is from my own school days. An inspirational teacher introduced me and the rest of my Year 6 class to the difficult word of the day. She challenged us to discuss its meaning, find ways of using it in the work set out for the day and define its meaning in artwork, stories and other curriculum learning. The one that sticks in mind to this day is the word silhouette. Discovering its meaning and its visual magic was an inspiration, we looked at paintings, pictures and even created our own silhouettes using tissue paper. We wrote poetry and considered how haunting a silhouette looks in the gloom or the moonlight.

A deeper focus on comprehension

Comprehension skills are an essential part of developing fluency in reading. Recognising the key vocabulary that a pupil will encounter when reading a text whether it is fiction or non-fiction is a fundamental first step. The teacher needs to be aware of the words that may be unfamiliar or difficult to decode. It is a good idea to have to hand the three tiers of vocabulary defined by Dr Isabel Beck, Dr Margaret McKeown, and Dr Linda Kucan in the 2002 publication of their book titled *Bringing Words to Life*.

Within the EYFS framework communication and literacy are two of the key areas for learning and development. There is an emphasis on developing a wide vocabulary through the spoken word and through pupils being read to as much as possible. Creating opportunities for a two-way conversation between the child and the adult from an early age are the foundations for language and cognitive development.

This continues to be a key feature of the programme of study for English at Key Stage 1. It is the layering of learning that is easy to miss from the way the documents are put together in a linear fashion. For instance, in Year 1 the standard says that pupils should listen to and discuss a wide range of poems, stories and non-fiction and link what they read to their own experiences. By Year 2 the standard is looking to ensure that pupils can express views about the materials they are reading. They are also expected to be able to discuss the sequence of events in books and how items of information are related. In building these skills over the span of more than one year the teacher has to skilfully focus on ensuring that all pupils can make sense of the texts they are exposed to, understand and decode the vocabulary and have the skills to express an opinion or recognise sequencing.

Lower Key Stage 2 takes this sequencing a step further and the standard requires the teacher to provide books that are structured in a different way and provide materials that allow for pupils to read for a range of purposes. Pupils are also encouraged by this stage to recommend books that they have read to their peers, giving reasons for their choices. By the end of lower Key Stage 2 pupils should be able to demonstrate their comprehension of the written work across several genres and be able to read aloud and perform showing understanding through intonation, tone and volume so that meaning is clear to an audience.

Upper Key Stage 2 creates further challenges for the developing reader and their teacher. Continuing to read widely across several genres, pupils should also now be beginning to identify and discuss themes and conventions in and across their reading. They should also be able to explain and discuss their understanding through formal presentations and debates with their peers and adults and show how they can maintain a focus linked to the topic or subject matter.

Layering this ability to comprehend and build a deep vocabulary will create for the pupil a foundation that will last them a lifetime. It is, however, essential that teachers have the right training and understand how to support pupils to develop these skills incrementally and create the opportunities for them to revisit, recall and practise through a variety of reading material both fiction and non-fiction.

Many teachers may not have any formal training in the art of comprehension. Their own English learning may well have ended when they were 16 with GCSE or 18 if they studied English to A Level. The PGCE is a short course of a mere nine months and although a focus on primary education will undoubtedly cover sessions on literacy, a deep trawl into the essential development of comprehension of the written word may not be possible.

It is, therefore, important that there is a whole-school focus on ensuring teachers can work collaboratively to develop a deep understanding of the National Curriculum standards (DfE, 2013) that sequence the development of effective reading and clearly examine how that can be achieved. Bringing teachers together from across the year groups to unpick the standards and determine a sequence of learning may be time consuming but it will reap so many benefits it should be an essential element of timetabling and planning.

Here are the seven must teach comprehension strategies that can be overlayed onto the standards or programmes of study for EYFS, Key Stage 1 and Key Stage 2 (EYFS, 2021; Using recall and prior knowledge

1   Making connections
2   Predicting
3   Inferring
4   Questioning
5   Monitoring
6   Visualising
7   Summarising

Creating opportunities for teachers from across the primary phases to plan together using these principles and that takes account of the sequence of learning set out in the programmes of study allows them to focus on the kinds of pedagogical approaches that will support pupils to be unconsciously competent readers who love to read for pleasure, to deepen their understanding and to make sense of their place in the world.

For example, using recall and prior knowledge is there as a standard in the Year 1 programme of study 'Become familiar with key stories, fairy tales and traditional tales, retelling these and considering their characteristics'. In Year 2 pupils are expected to be able to 'Recognise simple recurring literacy language'. In Year 3, there must be evidence that pupils 'Recognise some different forms of poetry'; by Year 6 they should be able to 'Explain and discuss their understanding of what they have read, including through formal presentations and debates, maintaining a focus on topic and using notes where necessary (Baker and Brown, 1984).

Other strategies are also clearly evident within the language used in the curriculum standards. 'Discuss favourite words and phrases' allows pupils to show that they can infer their meaning and make connections as to where they are used within the text. 'Listening to, discussing and expressing views about a wide range of poetry, stories and non-fiction' or 'Reading books that are structured in different ways and reading for a range of purposes' allows pupils to make connections, summarise their understanding and question the reasons why certain texts are more relevant in certain contexts.

There is a clear sequence to how a pupil gently and carefully deepens their ability to read and understand. Teachers need to share their approaches to how they teach to the standard, how they assess the depth of pupils' ability to comprehend what they are reading and how they capture a passion for the written word. None of this can happen if teachers remain isolated in their own classrooms without the opportunity to learn from other teachers and can celebrate good and best practice. We focus in more detail on sequencing of the curriculum in Chapter 6.

I also like the five Ps of comprehension designed by Carol Aston and Dr Pat Stafford (2010):

- Points of view
- Patterns and connections
- Puzzles
- Predictions
- Possibilities

Writing – a record of our thoughts, ideas, proof of understanding or a repository for knowledge

Writing is the coin of the realm, the currency in which ideas are most widely circulated and valued. (Lemov, 2016)

It is quite deliberate that I have chosen to write about writing after looking into the essential skills of oracy and reading. If we want our children to write well then it is essential that they are firstly exposed to other forms of communication that will stimulate their interest and allow them to develop ideas and formulate in their minds what it is they want to write about. Writing is the product of learning as far as assessing that learning is concerned and is therefore often given much higher consideration than the other skills associated with literacy and English.

Writing is complex and requires pupils firstly to be able to decode words, put them into sentences and then make meaning out of disjointed facts and information. The formal act of writing requires the writer to put their thoughts and ideas into something that can be understood by others.

Thoughts are hidden, the spoken word is transient and usually not recorded. When pupils write they have to deliberately form into words what they want to convey about themselves, about their understanding of a topic or a specific curriculum theme or that allows them to create a world of their own. This can be exposing and many pupils may be put off by the fact that their writing is overtly assessed not for its quality but for spelling mistakes, punctuation errors or grammar misuse.

The curriculum standards in The National Curriculum Programmes of Study for English Key Stage 1 and 2 (2014) clearly outline the sequence by which pupils should develop proficiency, fluidity and originality in the way they learn to write. Once again, the advice must be to create the opportunity for all staff from across the year groups to look at the sequencing that builds the skills associated with writing. Even in early years the Early Years Foundation Stage (EYFS) framework document (March 2021) expects that pupils will 'write simple phrases and sentences that can be read by others'.

What is taught in terms of structure and sequencing is carefully laid out in some detail from year to year. Teachers need the time and the opportunity to work together to dovetail the learning so that there is explicit evidence that pupils can build on their prior learning and achievement and continue to develop and grow in their ability to write. It is, evidently, not possible to create such precise and clearly defined layers of learning in oracy or reading but writing allows us to assess a strong grasp or otherwise of a variety of definable standards. These include spelling, word structure, handwriting, grammar and punctuation. Writing for effect is not a standard but to me is the essence of why we must teach our children to see the written word as a powerful way to be expressive, independent and aware of the world and how they can contribute to its and their future prosperity.

For instance, the aims documented at the beginning of the statutory requirements for writing are as follows:

- Year 1 – Encode sounds and develop the physical skill needed for handwriting
- Year 2 – Compose individual sentences orally and then write them down. Spell correctly many of the words covered in Year 1. Make phonically plausible attempts to spell words

they have not yet learnt. Form individual letters correctly, so establishing good handwriting habits from the beginning
- Year 3 and 4 – Write down ideas with a reasonable degree of accuracy and with good sentence punctuation. Teachers should therefore be consolidating pupils' writing skills, their vocabulary, their grasp of sentence structure and their knowledge of linguistic terminology
- Year 5 and 6 – Write down ideas quickly. Grammar and punctuation should be broadly accurate. Spelling of most words taught so far should be accurate and they should be able to spell words that they have not yet been taught by using what they have learnt about how spelling works in English and reflect their understanding of the audience for and purpose of their writing by selecting appropriate vocabulary and grammar

The above is a snapshot of a much more detailed statutory structure within the English programmes of study and provides a clear pattern of what is expected across the two key stages. The emphasis on technical knowledge of word structures, grammar and punctuation as well as spelling must not be ignored. However, using the widest possible opportunities to encourage writing for pleasure for different audiences and for many different purposes across the curriculum will help to develop a love of writing and ensure that all pupils have the skills in readiness for the next stage of their education, their secondary school.

Conceptual maths and fluency in numeracy

The maths curriculum is set out to create a systematic opportunity for pupils to develop increased fluency in mathematical competence year by year. The aims for the curriculum are explicit and want pupils to become fluent in the fundamentals of mathematics, reason mathematically and solve problems by applying maths concepts in a variety of routine and non-routine problems.

Once again, the need to create opportunities for those who teach maths on a daily basis in the primary school to demonstrate that they are building on prior learning and know the sequence of learning that will lead to pupils achieving specific standards at the end of each year and each key stage is essential.

There is a clear requirement to focus on the vocabulary of number and mathematics. Maths has a language of its own and as well as words that may have several meanings there are also symbols, images, tables and graphs. Where pupils find the language of maths difficult, they may also find the maths itself problematic. It is therefore important to ensure that pupils have the opportunity to access the meaning of words used within the context of mathematical learning. Words such as score, acute, degree, estimate, fraction, combine, margin, square, quantum, negative, integer, infinite, factor and divide can have meanings in other subjects or in other contexts.

Teaching the concepts that underpin the explicit teaching of mathematics in a systematic way is essential. Pupils need to have the opportunity to develop competence in the use of numeracy skills across the range of different mathematical disciplines including, number, fractions, measurement, geometry and statistics. There is a clear stepped progression within the statutory guidance for each year across the two key stages and for each discipline. For instance, decimals appear within the guidance for fractions in Year 4 and percentages in Year 5.

Seeing the progression through the maths curriculum is important but then so is ensuring that pupils master the basics, develop their conceptual understanding and begin to relate and make connections across elements of their learning as they are able to work with increasingly complex mathematical processes. Some pupils will inevitably find this easier than others. Differentiating the content within the maths curriculum is therefore vital to ensuring all pupils achieve and progress through the statutory maths curriculum and can demonstrate that they have mastery at each stage of their learning (Drury, 2015).

Assessment of the learning must be an integral part of the planning and the pedagogy. Where pupils fail to grasp the concept, where there are misconceptions and misunderstandings, there is every possibility that the pupil will be held back and eventually lead to confusion, fear and a life-long belief that maths is beyond them. Weaving what and how the learning will be assessed to ensure that pupils have arrived at the end points that have been planned for is an essential element of planning for all subjects but in maths it is particularly important. Maths can be fun, it is about patterns, codes, depth and shape and is the essence of our world. Making it accessible for all pupils has a massive impact on learning in all subjects and elsewhere beyond school.

Maths in context across the curriculum

It is my experience that in many primary schools maths remains the domain of the maths lesson. It is understandable that time is devoted to the teaching of maths as a discrete subject. There is a lot to cover and it takes time and lots of revision, reflection and rote learning to develop and form the mathematical brain and create the right conditions for concepts to remain within the long-term memory as a conduit for even more complex learning and problem-solving. Many teachers may themselves feel a lack of confidence and have to work hard to teach a subject that they have struggled with themselves. It is, therefore, often contained within carefully structured sterile lessons where achievement is a series of right answers or an understanding that certain pupils didn't quite get it.

Maths is everywhere. The classroom would be a dangerous structure if it were not for the calculations made to hold up the roof, the windows and doors have to adhere to stringent measurement of angles and the properties that make them the shape they are. Football wouldn't be football if we didn't have tables and graphs, the excitement of goal difference and the desperate counting of the minutes of extra time. The preparation of food would be a disaster if we didn't understand ratio, temperature and quantity. There is a wonder and symmetry to the arc of a rainbow, the circular nature of a flower and the way the petals are arranged. When we show pupils from an early age the wonder of maths and the way maths is everywhere and is essential to our very being we begin to bring an understanding of why we need to learn mathematical concepts, facts and processes.

There are so many examples of where maths is integral to the learning within science and across all of the other foundation subjects. Even in English there is a wealth of opportunities to see what has been taught in a maths lesson brought to life as part of a story, an account or a description.

There is a myriad of opportunities to reinforce the learning from maths lessons. Pupils can practice in a context, learn through meaningful problem-solving and make connections that will help them to retain their learning ready for the next complex maths problem to tackle.

Here are some more examples:

- Making pastry requires an understanding of the ratio between fat and flour
- Creating a pie chart helps to compare the population of different EU countries
- Plotting a graph of rainfall captured over time can be part of a weather study
- Deciding on the shape of a bird table roof and measuring the angles reinforces learning about triangles
- Measuring when a liquid turns to a solid is a maths skill in science
- Using a thermometer to measure changes in temperature can be plotted on a graph
- Comparing the population of London in 1666 with now can be very revealing
- Using a stopwatch to compare how quickly members of a team run their race
- Using scale in geography to work out the distance between one point and another

These are just some examples and more could be added. When specific maths concepts are taught, if there are ways these can be immediately used to demonstrate their relevance in a real-life situation such as using triangles to strengthen the bird table roof or capturing data in an experiment that can then be turned into a graph it helps pupils to consolidate their learning.

The essence here is to reinforce the mathematical understanding and re-visit the mathematical vocabulary across the full range of foundation subjects. If this doesn't happen it is a missed opportunity to build a much more profound understanding of mathematics. It is, however, important not to turn an exciting lesson of discovery into just another maths lesson. It is the application of the numeracy skill in the pursuance of deeper knowledge across subjects that must be the emphasis and, wow, what a difference it makes. I can only avow to the many light bulb moments I have witnessed where the essential maths concept is brought to life.

Creating the thinking and metacognitive skills that lead to reflection, reciprocity, reasoning and resilience

> Metacognition and self-regulation approaches aim to help pupils think about their own learning more explicitly, often by teaching them specific strategies for planning, monitoring and evaluating their learning. Interventions are usually designed to give pupils a repertoire of strategies to choose from and the skills to select the most suitable strategy for a given task.
>
> (Education Endowment Foundation (EEF) (2018)
> *Metacognition and Self-Regulated Learning*)

So far in this chapter we have looked at the essential core skills for learning, literacy and numeracy. We cannot simply leave it there as it is a range of other skills that will create the right conditions for learning and create for the learner many opportunities to understand how they learn as well as what they learn.

There are three components that create opportunities for self-regulated learning. They are amplified in Figure 4.1.

Cognition is the mental process involved in knowing, understanding and learning. Stimulating the brain is a pretty obvious necessity in the function of learning. Pupils also need exposure and practice in a range of metacognitive skills where they are effectively 'learning how to learn'. In order to create the self-regulated learner, we also must create the right conditions whereby our pupils are willing to learn and are motivated to want to continue to seek out new learning and experiences.

Understanding metacognition is an imperative to innovative pedagogy. Knowing the skills that pupils need to extend their repertoire of knowledge and learn in different ways will create the responsive and skilful learner who absorbs knowledge, makes connections across their learning and becomes unconsciously competent in the use of the many and varied skills that will allow them to become life-long learners.

These skills for learning include developing a progressive understanding of how to work independently and in groups, how to infer, argue and debate using subject content and a wide range of powerful vocabulary, study skills that allow learning to take place without the presence of the teacher, taking on challenges and accepting change, responding to feedback and being self-reflective and planning and managing learning strategies.

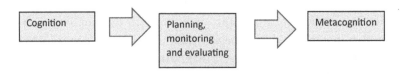

Figure 4.1 From facts to deepening knowledge and understanding

There are many and varied ways that teachers can support their pupils to learn how to learn, essentially promoting active learning that is pupil-centred. These include:

- Encouraging pupils to plan, monitor and evaluate their own learning
- Create opportunities for pupils to reflect on their achievements and what they can do to improve
- Promote classroom dialogue and encourage all pupils to be a part of a learning community
- Use open and challenging questioning to build confidence and foster challenge
- Coach pupils towards independence and a self-belief that will leave them less reliant on the teacher
- Use modelling to aid understanding and encourage pupils to model their learning to others

Below are a series of questions that may be a starting point for teachers to reflect on their own pedagogy and to what extent they are helping their pupils towards an understanding of how they learn and how they can develop the metacognitive skills that will ensure they are learning how to be life-long learners who are curious, who absorb knowledge and who are encouraged to reflect on their own abilities and strategies for continuous improvement.

- How can you encourage pupils to share and collaborate about their learning in pairs and in groups?
- What are the strategies that help to activate prior knowledge to develop a deeper understanding of a new topic?
- How do you create opportunities for pupils to work independently to find out more, deepen their understanding or broadening their knowledge?
- Where are the opportunities that ensure pupils are reading widely both fiction and non-fiction to reinforce their comprehension skills?
- How do you encourage pupils to talk about and be aware of their strengths and how they can build on these to learn more?
- How are pupils encouraged to plan their learning linked to clearly defined learning goals?
- What are the strategies that support pupils to monitor their own progress towards achieving their learning goals?
- How can you raise awareness of the importance of effective listening as a skill for learning?
- What are the strategies that ensure there is sufficient and appropriate challenge that encourages pupils to find solutions and be prepared to fail in the pursuit of learning?
- To what extent do you value effort as part of the journey towards successful learning?
- How often are pupils encouraged to reflect on their learning and focus on the learning strategies they use to support their learning?

The Education Endowment Foundation has undertaken some very comprehensive research into metacognition and their seven-step guide is an invaluable source of information for all teachers and curriculum planners. We cannot teach the curriculum effectively without a focus on metacognition, as their study points out in section 2, 'The clue is in the phrase: *without cognition, there is no metacognition*' (EEF, 2018). Learning requires a thorough grounding in subject knowledge and the skills to absorb and use that subject knowledge. It is therefore essential to look at each topic, subject or theme and determine the skills – both the core literacy and numeracy skills and the wider thinking skills – and share with pupils how these skills will support them to deepen their knowledge, understand that there are connections and similarities in a lot of their learning and create for them a thirst for more.

Conclusion

Literacy and numeracy are the bedrock of teaching in the primary school. The EYFS framework creates the starting point for ensuring pupils begin their learning with a deep focus on the basics of oracy, reading, writing and simple maths and numeracy. Throughout Key Stage 1 and 2 the English and maths programmes of study lead the teacher through a sequence of progressive learning that will hopefully equip pupils with a range of skills that will prepare them for the next stage in their education. It is essential that all teachers are deeply familiar with the statutory requirements within these documents or have a similar set of standards that will ensure pupils have the same opportunities that lead to readiness for Key Stage 3 and beyond.

Knowledge, it is argued, is the key to successful learning and it is. However, without the fundamental basics developed over time, practised and revisited, pupils will not be able to access deep knowledge and make sense of it. For all teachers who have the privilege to teach in this arena they also need to focus on the wider thinking skills, the metacognitive skills that knit the learning together and that create for pupils opportunities to share their thoughts with peers and with other adults. Also, to gain skills in how to plan their learning, learn fluency and pace, and develop the skills of enquiry, note-taking and sifting and selecting relevant information. Teachers must be given time to plan together, to share their experiences of helping pupils to learn as well as some of the issues that might stop learning taking place. Teachers need to challenge their own pedagogy, question the status quo and continue to look for ways to improve through positive interaction, learning conversations and professional reflection. This is an important and pivotal chapter and without the skills it discusses no one can expect to access and make sense of the myriad of knowledge there is to learn.

Top tips

- For all teachers who teach in the primary phase there is an imperative to look to the Early Years Foundation Stage framework (March 2021) in order to determine how to plan so that there is clear evidence that pupils are building on their prior learning
- Teachers in Key Stage 1 should work together to create curriculum maps that define the skills pupils need to develop as part of their learning. Also, teachers should work together as lower Key Stage 2 and upper Key Stage 2 to build on the learning sequentially
- Planning linked to curriculum implementation must take account of the rationale and ambition the school has defined as part of its vision and intent for continuing improvement and high-quality outcomes for all pupils
- Focusing on what pupils need to know and can do by the end of Year 6 is an excellent place to start in planning backwards to plot the sequence of learning
- Creating opportunities to reinforce literacy and numeracy skills as an intrinsic element of deepening knowledge across all foundation subjects will build unconscious competence
- See speaking and listening (oracy) as essential elements of planning for deep learning across all subjects. Talk improves reading, writing and understanding
- Take account of the bulleted list in the English programme of study of what should be achieved between Years 1 and 6 in relation to speaking and listening and refine pedagogy linked to their implementation
- Focus on the aims within the English programme of study for Key Stage 1 and 2 to reflect on the importance of reading across a range of fiction and non-fiction genre
- Comprehension is a key pedagogy in all subjects not just in English. Complete an audit to find out how many teachers know how to teach comprehension explicitly
- Focus on writing as an explicit skill where pupils plan what they are going to write, talk about it first and are encouraged to write fluidly and with passion
- Create as many opportunities as possible to re-emphasise maths conceptual learning where it is an essential part of deepening knowledge across the foundation subjects
- Metacognition or learning how to learn needs explicit attention in order to help pupils develop a range of skills associated with learning and to motivate pupils to want to learn

References

Aston, C., and Stafford, P. Dr. (2010) *Learning Unleashed*. London: ASA Education Limited.

Baker, L. and Brown, A. L. (1984) *Metacognitive Skills and Reading*. Technical Report No. 188. Urbana, IL: Illinois University Center for the Study of Reading.

Beck, I. L., McKeown, M. G. and Kucan, L. (2002) *Bringing Words to Life*. New York: Guildford Press.

Department for Education (DfE) (2013) *National Curriculum Programmes of Study in England*. London: DfE.

Department for Education (DfE) (2014) *National Curriculum Programme of Study for English Key Stage 1 and 2*. London: DfE.

Department for Education (DfE) (2021) *Statutory Framework for the Early Years Foundation Stage*. London: DfE.

Drury, H. (2015) *Mastering Mathematics: Teaching to Transform Achievement*. Oxford: Oxford University Press.

Education Endowment Foundation (2018) *Metacognition and Self-Regulated Learning*. London: Education Endowment Foundation.

Lemov, D. (2016) *Reading Reconsidered*. San Francisco: Jossey-Bass.

Myatt, M. (2018) *The Curriculum: Gallimaufry to Coherence*. Woodbridge: John Catt Educational.

Paris, S. G., Wasik, B. A. and Turner, J. C. (1991) 'The Development of Strategies of Readers'. In Barr, R., Kamil, M., Mosenthal, P. and Pearson, P. D. (eds), *Handbook of Reading Research*, (Vol. 2), pp. 609–40. Mahwah, NJ: Lawrence Erlbaum Associates.

University of Cambridge (2018) *Voice 21 and Oracy Cambridge*.

Williams, J. C. (2013) *Towards a Standards Based Curriculum: A Toolkit for the New Primary Curriculum in England*. London: Publish Nation.

5

CONCEPTS AND SUBJECT KNOWLEDGE: CREATING SUBJECT-SPECIFIC AND CROSS-CURRICULAR CONNECTIONS

A concept-based curriculum teaches broad concepts like change, balance, identity and systems. It recognises that facts and topics are important elements of learning, but that there are other levels of learning above them that we can define and design. It shows how one level of learning informs the next, and how students can transfer knowledge within a subject, between subjects, and even between school and the world around them.

(Chalk.com, 2021)

The principles of conceptual learning and its place in the primary curriculum

There is a great deal of time and astounding opportunity to use the two years of the Early Years Foundation Stage (EYFS) learning and the six years of primary schooling to create for pupils a rich tapestry of learning that truly equips them for the next stage of their education. The curriculum is a series of subjects that create opportunities for the learner to access a rich seam of knowledge and a deeper understanding of the world they are born into and will inherit as part of their future. Each subject stands alone as a discipline and there are principles that academic experts have used to shape subject content in relation to the knowledge that the learner should have within that discipline. How this translates into a determination to teach a deep and broad curriculum in the primary phase needs careful consideration.

The role of the primary school is to prepare pupils for the next stage of their education, to ensure they have the basic core skills of speaking, listening, reading, writing and mathematics and a whole range of wider thinking skills that will allow them to grow as positive citizens. The primary curriculum is the blueprint that defines what should be taught and how through outstanding pedagogy learning takes place over a time span from Year 1 to Year 6. The aim is to ensure pupils acquire a body of subject knowledge across the specified subjects, a wide vocabulary and the social skills that will ensure pupils are active members of their school and wider communities (Blatchford, 2013).

Acquiring subject knowledge across different disciplines where learning is processed and remembered as pupils move from year to year and key stage to key stage is problematic. One-hour lessons, the subject divides, new teachers in each new year group and large classes can be a recipe for piecemeal learning with few connections made and the deepening of knowledge highly unlikely. This can then lead to criticism from secondary school subject leaders and experts bemoaning the lack of learning, dearth of knowledge and poor core skills.

The answer to this criticism has to be in a deep focus on the curriculum as a whole where conceptual learning is an integral part of the long- and medium-term planning process. Each subject has its own core of knowledge, but each subject is also bound by the concepts that explore and explain that knowledge and how it changes perception, explains cause and effect, explores similarities and differences and determines sources in a wide variety of contexts. The vocabulary that defines the term concepts is rich with possibilities and creates for the teacher and for the pupil opportunities to be creative, analytical and perceptive.

Defining concepts within subjects and across the curriculum

Concepts link meaning and create a way of making sense of learning in different subjects. For instance, the automobile or car to most of us these days is a simple concept we take for granted. The fact that there is a myriad of different makes, designs, colours and engines that make up a wide variety of types of car, the term car is still a term we can all relate to and understand its generic meaning.

Across the curriculum in each subject there are many different concepts. The example above relating to a car is a concrete example of a concept. It is visual, simple and will be recognisable to everyone. Other similar concrete examples of concepts could include, animals, plants, trees, countries and so on. There are other concepts that are more abstract and are the ones that can make a significant difference to how pupils learn the knowledge within a subject and across a range of themes that transcend specific subjects. Examples might include source, beliefs, power, invasion, light, osmosis. They are immediately relevant in certain subject contexts but equally can transcend subject disciplines and provide the teacher and the pupil with an opportunity to make connections across the curriculum that will help to cement that learning over time.

Concepts are a feature of all curricula across the whole spectrum of education. The importance within the primary school is to recognise that concepts exist within and across subjects and will be the key to rich learning opportunities that will support the development of increasing depth and breadth of knowledge and understanding. Teachers should be encouraged through explicit subject-specific CPD to focus on the prevalence of concepts in subjects that they will be teaching. Concrete and simple concepts are fairly obvious – plants are a simple concept figure in the science curriculum in each year from Early Years to Year 6. Habitat and temperature are more complex concepts introduced in Year 2. Classification, another complex concept, is introduced in Year 3 and 4, while in Year 5 and 6 reproduction is a new complex concept that is the final part of the sequence of learning about plants and animals.

It is important that teachers focus on the concepts which are key to helping pupils to understand and deepen the knowledge within the subject they are learning about. For very young children it may be that the key concepts are simple and focus on, for instance, the plants they are growing themselves or can observe in their local environment. Their classification or habitat may not be relevant in the beginning and if introduced too soon may lead to cognitive overload.

For teachers, this opportunity is profound in allowing them to look in detail at subject-specific knowledge and how best to create a plan from Early Years (EYFS Framework, 2021) to Year 6 and beyond that sequences the learning to gradually introduce the more complex and essential understanding that comes with the introduction of more abstract concepts.

Examining the potential of conceptual learning in a post-pandemic era

There was probably little or no opportunity for pupils to focus on conceptual learning during the time they have been home schooled or attending school where normal lessons with their own teacher were not possible. It will take a long time to redress the balance and ensure that for all pupils' learning is not lost. It is through positive and highly innovative pedagogical approaches and a continued focus on conceptual learning as well as subject knowledge that will help to fill any gaps in learning and reinforce where pupils have gained new and relevant perspectives.

Where teachers are developing their own understanding of conceptual learning, they can plan how to assess what pupils know, understand and need to revisit. Where teachers work with their pupils using discussion, they can assess how much pupils have absorbed and what they are missing in terms of their conceptual understanding of the subject they are learning. Where teachers work together to highlight the key concepts within their discipline, they are developing strategies for how and when to introduce concepts that will aid understanding. It is likely that for many pupils working from home the emphasis has been on information and facts which are much more accessible without a teacher present. However, this can mean that the learning is shallow and is therefore only remembered in the short term.

Focusing on how those facts interrelate with specific concepts will support deeper understanding and help to ensure the retention of the facts as knowledge. We must also remember that remote learning does not provide the teacher with the opportunity to seek out where pupils have misunderstood or developed the wrong understanding where misconception is the result. Where teachers have a clear picture of the concepts that wrap around the subject matter, they can probe deeply using challenging questioning techniques to establish if pupils have misconceptions as a result of a lack of contact with the teacher. Misconception inevitably acts as a barrier to future learning so a strategy that establishes for all subject experts the key concepts within their area of expertise will highlight where there are problems.

Long-term planning using concepts to create curriculum breadth and depth

Concepts are evident within the aims and statutory requirements of all the programmes of study that make up the curriculum in both the foundation and core subjects.

Table 5.1 shows a list of some of the key abstract concepts that appear in subjects across the curriculum. This is taken from a simple trawl through each National Curriculum programme of study for Key Stage 1 and 2. This list is broadly subject/faculty-specific. However, many of the concepts transcend subjects such as sources, which could relate to the sources of a river, the source material that leads to evidence about a period in history, the source of raw materials needed to make a product or the source of information leading to decisions to be made.

Table 5.1 Curriculum concepts within broad subject themes

Humanities	Science and Computer Science	Creative arts
Civilisation, culture, empire, invasion, monarchy, tyranny, rebellion, oppression, politics, religion, society, community, taxation, source, evidence, chronology, royalty, beliefs, ideologies, customs, artefacts, hierarchy, diocese, traditions, authority, atmosphere, climate, continent, landform, terrain, settlement, population, region, trade, development, sustainability, diversity, inclusion	Methods, processes, forces, rational explanation, characteristics, terminology, nature, enquiry, patterns, light, plants, trees, classification, data analysis, graphical, synthesis, experimenting structure, principles, abstraction, logic, digital content, algorithms, information technology, analysis, manipulation, programs, ranking, software, hardware, systems, responsibility	Dimensions, symmetry, accuracy, artists, genre, perspective, materials, design, drawing, painting, sculpture, technique, media, craft, sketch, language, history, creativity, expression, composition, performance, tempo, timbre, texture, structure, notation, control, fluency, singing, sound, play
PE and Design Technology	**SMSC and Cultural Capital**	**Where are these taken from?**
Skills, flexibility, technique, challenge, control, teamwork, strategy, opposition, competence, physical activity, competition, accuracy, agility, co-ordination, tactics, performance, design, make, function, product, quality, prototype, principles, nutrition, construction, properties, mechanics, ingredients, materials, components, systems, planning	Choices, rights, needs, behaviour, opinions, debate, environment, money, personal hygiene, differences, similarities, emotions, health, well-being, identity, relationships, health, risk, change, human rights, rule of law, culture	Taken as a result of a trawl through the National Curriculum Programmes of Study for key stage 1 and 2. Many of the words or concepts can be used in the context of other subjects than the ones they are attributed to. However, in the main these words are there in the specific programmes of study stated here providing a rich vein of vocabulary.

Curriculum concepts within broad subject themes

There is no definitive list of concepts and nor should there be but having something as a starting point will be useful certainly for teachers and subject leaders who lack deep subject expertise and who may lack confidence in developing schemes of work or teaching concepts as part of their repertoire.

Creating the right conditions for planning the curriculum requires some systematic thought and a collective body of knowledge and understanding. The following list needs to be a part of the initial design:

- Start with a clear view of the end points you want from pupils to achieve by the time they leave primary school
- Define the ambition for pupils linked to what you want pupils to learn including knowledge, skills and their conceptual understanding
- Focus on a clear and sequenced plan that dovetails the subject content from year to year including skills development (Chapter 4 will help here)
- Ensure that there are opportunities for pupils to build on their prior learning, deepen their learning, revisit and reflect on their learning and share their understanding with others
- Have a clear plan for how to work with those pupils who need a challenge or extra help or where it is clear there are gaps in their learning
- Know the vocabulary of each subject both for simple concepts and more abstract concepts
- Assessment must be a part of the planning process – what will be assessed, when assessment will take place and how learning will be assessed
- Define the cross-curricular similarities and differences and ensure that there are carefully crafted opportunities to share these with pupils

The curriculum is the fulcrum by which the quality of both pedagogy and learning outcomes can be defined and assessed. Where there is a commitment from leaders within the school to create the right conditions for joint planning to take place, subject and phase leaders and their teams have an opportunity to look at the curriculum as a whole and not just as fragments from different subjects and different years. Where subjects are taught in isolation and there is no continuity or positive communication across year groups the result is poorer outcomes in the way pupils learn and progress. Where the curriculum is seen as a continuum not just within the subject but across the subject divides a very clear pathway to a clearly defined sequence of learning emerges. The teacher understands what pupils should already know, what they need to learn in order to deepen their knowledge and which strategies in terms of recall, reflection and retrieval need to be incorporated along the way (Young and Lambert, 2014). For subject leaders and their teams an understanding of the concepts that define the subject can provide a rich vein of understanding of the significant knowledge and vocabulary contained in each subject.

Addressing the lack of subject expertise for some primary teachers

Research suggests that primary school teachers do not have the relevant subject expertise across the range of subjects they are expected to teach. This is certainly emphasised in a piece of research undertaken by the Education Department of the University of Cambridge. Their findings suggested that it was difficult for trainee teachers to access teaching practice within the foundation subjects as many of their host schools mainly focused on teaching English, maths and science with a very piecemeal approach to teaching the foundation subjects. Opportunities to develop explicit skills in geography, history or music and art were patchy with good or best practice rarely evident. The new curriculum introduced in 2014 was meant to address this with a move from a skills-focused to a more knowledge-led curriculum model.

At the time of writing there is still a distinct lack of deep subject expertise in primary teachers and little or no CPD to address this. The opportunity to focus on professional learning within school or across a group of schools that looks in detail at the language that defines subject curricula from Early Years to Year 6 and even into Key Stage 3 provides a real opportunity to focus on concepts that seal the learning for pupils.

Being mindful of cognitive load, it is not necessary to delve too deeply into the theory that underpins an academic study of the possible characteristics of strong teaching and learning linked to subject expertise (Young, 2018). However, a short dive into some of the terms linked to conceptual learning might help to unpick what teachers should focus on in identifying the key concepts they need to highlight and when to teach them.

Firstly, we should have a look at the terms disciplinary and substantive knowledge. The curriculum is designed with discrete subjects at its heart from Key Stage 1 onwards. The content of each subject is decided upon in education circles a long way from the primary school, in universities and subject associations. However, a simple explanation of these two definitions is useful in explaining why the subjects are defined as individual 'disciplines' even in the context of the primary school. Let's start with substantive knowledge, which is the factual content for the subject and which must be connected into a careful sequence. So, for example, where pupils are learning about volcanoes, they need a lot more than just the word volcano. Where do they come from? What causes them to happen? Why do they happen when they do? What are their characteristics? Substantive knowledge therefore requires prior knowledge in order that pupils can learn over time a deeper understanding of volcanoes. Substantive knowledge most certainly embraces the idea that conceptual knowledge is an essential element of sequential and deep learning.

Disciplinary knowledge is linked to the procedures we need to learn in order to access knowledge. So, in history, in order to discuss facts we think we know about a period or event we need to have identified and referred to certain sources of evidence.

In science we need to have the ability to test out a hypothesis, in design we must be able to justify the reason for the need to make a product. Using the example of the volcano, the disciplinary knowledge would be an understanding of the mechanisms of the formation of a volcano and knowledge about what lies beneath the earth's crust before we can make substantive claims about the existence of volcanoes.

In this chapter we are looking at concepts so taking the idea of subject discipline a bit further we need to focus on *substantive concepts* which relate to the subject content so for instance in history this term would relate to words such as war, queen, century, or in geography words such as map, mountain, trade, population.

> Content, therefore, is important, not as facts to be memorised … but because without it students cannot acquire concepts and, therefore, will not develop their understanding and progress in their learning. (Young, 2018)

Alongside substantive concepts that underpin the nuts and bolts of the subject being studied we need to know about *second-order concepts* which provide the teacher with the means to organise subject knowledge and shape the way they teach in order to create for the pupil opportunities to use the simple but substantive concepts to organise and refine the subject knowledge. The teacher needs to be able to ask questions that bring the subject to life. For instance, the concept of a river in geography is simple but substantive; however, if we want our learners to know what happens to a river as it flows from its source to the sea then we need to think about flow, attrition, erosion and change, possibly leading to a question when studying a river in its youth and asking 'what is it about the flow of the river at this stage that affects the surrounding landscape?'

Substantive and second-order concepts are not specific to individual subjects and it is this rich cross-curricular vein that provides many opportunities to reinforce the learning, strengthen understanding of vocabulary and provide ways to support the pupil make connections that will help them to make sense of the knowledge they are acquiring. For instance, the River Thames in Tudor times played a valuable role as a route for transporting goods and prisoners to the Tower of London as well as people from place to place. The nature of the river's passage through its different stages is not relevant except to focus on the fact that it was deep enough for boats to navigate, slow flowing enough for people and goods to be safe and meandering enough to be easy to travel along. The second-order concepts here allow the teacher to ask deep and searching questions that link the learning to what was taught in geography and therefore reinforce the concept of how the river shapes the landscape and repeat the vocabulary that defines words like flow, depth, slow-moving and meandering.

The third type of concept it may be useful for the subject expert to learn about is the threshold concept. This is a concept that, once understood, modifies learners' understanding of a subject and opens doors into deeper learning and understanding.

Originally the study of threshold concepts comes from a research project into teaching and learning in undergraduate courses (Meyer and Land, 2003). They suggest that while 'core concepts' build on existing learning, layer by layer, threshold concepts open up new ways of thinking.

Threshold concepts once grasped are said to be irreversible, transformative and integrate with other learning and can be troublesome or difficult to grasp or hold onto. Such terms as photosynthesis can be viewed as a threshold concept. It is the process by which plants feed, thrive and excrete and is the starting point for a deeper understanding of the whole ecosystem that is things that grow. Evolution is another threshold concept within which a whole body of knowledge exists from the simple to the challenging. In maths we might be focusing on the concept of complex numbers and then breaking that concept down into their different component parts.

The essence here is for the subject leader and his or her team to focus on what are the central themes or key components of the learning in a particular topic or subject. Focusing less on the facts and detail and more on the key concepts allows the teacher to create more depth and opportunities for pupil-centred enquiry and problem-solving.

Simply put it means focusing on what is important about your subject. Let us return to my theme of looking at a river and its journey from source to sea where an abundance of concepts are essential for learning. The threshold concept here is that environments are changed by physical processes. This undeniable fact can then be the starting point for a study of volcanoes, earthquakes and coastal erosion to name but a few. It might also lead to the starting point for a discussion on why a Roman community chose a particular site to settle and build a town or the importance of the River Thames to London.

Practical strategies and subject-specific examples that might include conceptual learning

We have such great opportunities to build for our pupils during their time in the primary school a sense of wonder about their world and the place they occupy within it. Too often there is a narrow focus on subject knowledge and facts within each subject. Thinking about concepts allows the teacher to look beyond the simple factual knowledge and place it in a wider context or link it to a bigger picture. Facts on their own do not translate into knowledge, it is how they are interpreted, how pupils can make comparisons, see similarities and differences and build patterns that help to cement their learning.

In art, pupils need to learn how to paint, draw and sketch. This alone will not make them into artists or make sure they are discerning about the art they produce. Alongside developing skills as an artist, they need exposure to a range of artists and their work, to see different styles, what influenced the artist's choice of subject and in what period they lived and worked. There are also great opportunities to look for connections with other subjects, *The Last Moments of Lady Jane Grey* is an atmospheric and disturbing painting which is a great starting point for discussing a turbulent period in history. Art in religion is an opportunity for learning about understanding spirituality, incarnation, nativity, tradition and artifact. The focus on words such as symmetry and perspective create a whole world of possibilities in other subjects to use and find meaning – the symmetry in nature or the different perspectives of an argument.

Design technology is a rich vein for a deep focus on the conceptual nature of design. Making Egyptian urns or shields and swords that the Vikings might have used or even creating a street in order to burn it down to simulate the Great Fire of London are all regular outputs for design and technology (D&T) lessons. However, these are not providing a deep and meaningful look at the key aims of learning design and certainly will not create the perceptions pupils will need to develop if they are to thrive as designers in their secondary school and beyond. Design is a process that requires pupils to find a purpose for their inventiveness and skills in modelling. Building a pulley that will carry heavy weights, making a moving vehicle to go over rough terrain, making a cake that rises, designing and making a dress, a costume for the nativity or a school play that depicts the role of the wearer. All of these require a conceptual understanding of the principles of design as well as the skill of measuring, assembling and colouring in.

In geography and history, examples of which I have used earlier in this chapter, teachers must know the substantive and key concepts that underpin factual knowledge and breadth in learning. The development of deep, sequential understanding that builds for Early Years to Year 6 and then prepares pupils for further learning in Key Stage 3 and beyond relies on pupils developing underlying conceptual knowledge. For instance, there are many reasons for learning how to read a map that go beyond just knowing how to get from a to b. The map can help the pupil understand in more detail the reasons why settlements grow up and thrive because of the terrain, the presence of water and other resources. Sources of evidence in history are a rich vein of conceptual learning and provide the pupil with opportunities to look at articles, images, cartoons, artifacts, diary accounts or historic houses and gardens and begin to draw conclusions as to the reality of the past.

Maths does seem like it is all conceptual. However, knowing just how important some of the concepts in maths are for understanding is important. So, remember to focus on the concept of the prime number, or defining maths in terms of sets. Another interesting and complex concept is zero as a means of expressing nothing mathematically. In maths there are five elements of mathematical proficiency, including conceptual understanding; the others are procedural fluency, strategic competence, adaptive reasoning and communicating using symbols. In English all of the grammar terms are concepts and how we use them to really refine our ability to access and describe knowledge we are learning is crucial. This chapter could be endless if we start to unpick concepts in English literature. Let's leave that to the reader to focus on the books they have chosen as class readers, the poetry for study and the plays for reading or performing. It's a challenge but a good piece of professional learning for all those involved.

Planning for progression – the link between skills, knowledge and key concepts

Each subject is a combination of knowledge, skills and key concepts that bind the subject together. A balance between these three elements creates an opportunity to teach any subject to a depth that means the learning is progressive. Each of these three elements may dominate the process by which the learning will take place. For instance, when learning about the food chain in science, the starting point should be the facts around what exactly we mean by 'food chain'. We might then want to introduce some concepts that will help pupils to deepen their understanding of different food chains such as energy from the sun, for instance. All food chains start with a producer, another concept, which is a green plant that converts the sun's energy into food. A third concept might be a consumer and another a predator. Simple concepts linked to the subject of the food chain example might be used to aid understanding and cement the knowledge about food chains for a fish, a tiger, a butterfly and a bird.

Planning a sequence or unit of work over a period of, say, a few weeks needs careful thought. Simply focusing on the topic and factual outcomes misses opportunities to use concepts to bring the unit to life. Creating opportunities to use enquiry questions rather than presenting pupils with fact sheets or work sheets ensures that pupils are active rather than passive learners. So, in the Year 2 statutory requirements for science, pupils are expected to:

> Identify and compare the suitability of a variety of everyday materials, including wood, metal, plastic, glass, brick, rock, paper and cardboard for particular uses.
> (Department for Education (DfE) (2014) National Curriculum
> Programme of Study for Science in Year 2)

The enquiry task and associated questions could be asking which of the materials on the desk could you use to make a doll's house, a shed, a bird table, packaging for a present, as part of a garden, to cover food in the fridge. Providing the opportunity to touch, discuss and share ideas helps to ensure the learning is remembered, it provides an opportunity for pupils to immerse themselves in this task and builds their deeper knowledge and understanding. It provides the basis for further conceptual learning where the pupil will learn about the hardness and suitability of metals as well as where some materials are unsuitable for certain purposes. The combination of knowledge and concepts creates a strategy for deepening the learning over time.

The link between key concepts and knowledge is quite clear and it is the combination of these that will create for the pupil knowledge that is progressive and will be retained over time. However, without the skills to read, discuss, share ideas and write explanations that demonstrate that the pupil has, in fact, deepened their understanding, progress or learning is unlikely to happen. It is, therefore, essential to make sure that planning identifies the skills that pupils will use in the development of the series of lessons. These might include, what are the key factors involved in ensuring pupils can read the words that are part of the enquiry sequence as well as the enquiry question? How does the teacher know that the pupil has understood the conceptual terms such as soft, flammable or porous that they will need to have as part of their repertoire if they are to grasp the meaning of this particular learning exercise?

Planning that involves all three elements here will provide evidence of a rich vein of understanding of how pupils learn and how to ensure that what they learn is remembered and is then available for more learning and understanding. The learning in Year 2 is built upon in Year 5 where the statutory requirements in the science programme of study asks that pupils are taught to compare and group together everyday materials on the basis of their properties including hardness, solubility, transparency, conductivity. Where pupils are steered to their understanding of the suitability of certain products in Year 5, they are building on previous learning and understanding. They may need prompting and it may be that the teacher would want to revisit the previous learning in order to define some of the simple concepts so that pupils will find it easier when they are introduced to the more complex vocabulary of such concepts as transparency or conductivity. However, this is only possible if the Year 5 teacher knows what the Year 2 teacher was teaching so that comparisons can be made. Long- and medium-term planning that is recorded and shared is the only way to create progressive learning platforms.

> Could a curriculum be deliberately structured in order to ensure that prior knowledge is acquired and subsequently activated to secure new information? How might we construct a curriculum so that concepts in geography such as 'sustainability' and 'region' are understood, not as memorised definitions, but as well-connected schema with multiple contexts to add nuance to meaning and concrete examples to strengthen

the concept. The more nuanced the concept, the more likely it can be used to think critically. Our ability to think critically about sustainability, for example, will be greatly enhanced if we know about how sustainability has been attempted in several different contexts. (Percival, 2020)

Conclusion

Concepts may be something completely new to the primary teacher. Certainly, a trawl through some of the prospectuses for initial teacher training shows that conceptual learning is not a focus of their pathways to becoming a primary teacher. There is an agreement among many involved in initial teacher education that it is difficult to support primary teachers with explicit teaching practice that focuses on just having the opportunity to teach across a variety of the foundation subjects let alone delving into the different components of how to teach depth and breadth in acquiring knowledge and competence in a range of knowledge, concepts and skills. However, creating a culture where practising teachers understand the role of concepts in establishing strategies for deep learning will be evidence that there is a tacit understanding of how progression is measured and sustained over the six or so years a pupil spends learning in the primary phase.

Teachers should list the key concepts they believe are key to learning in their subject. There will be disagreement and different ideas that emerge. This is a positive outcome and aids deep understanding of the nature of the subjects under investigation. The programmes of study for each subject in the curriculum orders for England do provide opportunities to clearly see the difference between facts and concepts as well as the skills that are necessary for learning.

Teachers should work together to carefully document the concepts that are agreed are key to each subject. This could be in a scheme of work or a knowledge organiser, it might be a mind map or a fish diagram. Talking about the curriculum with subject specialists, identifying the main features and writing them down in a collective and progressive plan is probably the best CPD primary teachers will have had in a long time.

The way the primary curriculum is structured is through the statutory requirements for each individual subject, the core of English, maths and science and a range of individually defined foundation subjects. Senior leaders, curriculum planners and teachers must work together to structure the learning for pupils in a way that creates progression, depth of understanding and pupils who are unconsciously competent in a range of core and wider skills. Embracing a tacit understanding of the fact that the curriculum is a tapestry that weaves these elements together to create something that is a sum of its parts will be the evidence that every pupil is receiving the highest-quality learning experience.

--------------------------------- Top tips ---------------------------------

- Be clear as to the purpose and component parts of the primary curriculum
- Review the next stages of learning in specific subjects by knowing what is included in Key Stage 2 programmes of study for those planning for Key Stage 1 and the Key Stage 3 programme of study for those planning for Key Stage 2
- Create opportunities for subject leaders and teachers to work together to define the concepts within individual subjects
- Provide time for subject leaders and teachers to look at how some concepts are cross-curricular and provide opportunities for pupils to make connections across their learning in different subjects
- Beware of cognitive overload when introducing new concepts – there is a sequence to the approach to developing deep understanding and building knowledge that will stay in the long-term memory
- Find ways to establish where pupils might have gaps in their learning due to absence, school closures or other factors
- Think carefully about how to ask probing questions to challenge and to ascertain where there may be misconception or misunderstanding
- Create a vocabulary bank for each subject that is flexible and can be added to and shared with other subject specialists
- Create as many opportunities as possible for joint planning and CPD within and across key stages, subject groups and the whole school
- Accept that some subject leaders and teachers will not have the relevant knowledge and expertise and have a clearly defined plan as to how this can be addressed

References

Blatchford, R. (ed.) (2013) *Taking Forward the Primary Curriculum: Applying the 2014 National Curriculum for KS1 and KS2*. Woodbridge: John Catt Educational.

Chalk.com (2021) *Why Do You Need to Focus on Concept-Based Curriculum*. Available at: https://www.chalk.com/resources/concept-based-curriculum/ (accessed 27 July 2022).

Department for Education (DfE) (2014) *National Curriculum in England: Framework for Key Stages 1 and 2*. London: DfE.

Department for Education (DfE) (2014) *National Curriculum in England: Programme of Study for Science Key Stage 1 and 2*. London: DfE.

Department for Education (DfE) (2021) *Statutory Framework for the Early Years Foundation Stage*. London: DfE.

Meyer, J. H. F. and Land, R. (2003) 'Threshold concepts and troublesome knowledge: linkages to ways of thinking and practising'. In Rust, C. (ed.), *Improving Student Learning – Theory and Practice Ten Years On*. Oxford: Oxford Centre for Staff and Learning Development (OCSLD), pp. 412–24.

Percival, A. (2020) 'Curriculum Building in the Primary School'. In Sealy, C. (ed.) *The researchED Guide to The Curriculum*. Woodbridge: John Catt Educational.

Sealy, C. (ed.) (2020) *The researchED Guide to The Curriculum*. Woodbridge: John Catt Educational.

University of Cambridge Research Study (2015) *ITT and Practice in the Foundation Subjects*.

Young, M. (2018) 'A Knowledge-led curriculum: Pitfalls and possibilities'. *Impact* (4). Available at: https://my.chartered.college/impact_article/a-knowledge-led-curriculum-pitfalls-and-possibilities/ (accessed 27 July 2022).

Young, M. and Lambert, D. (2014) *Knowledge and the Future School*. London: Bloomsbury.

6

SEQUENCING THE LEARNING FOR DEPTH AND PROGRESSION

The very bones of our curriculum across the years and across subjects will need to link in a highly well thought out way, so that knowledge taught in one subject is explicitly reinforced and revisited not only in other subjects, but in subsequent years. In this way, key concepts and vocabulary are reinforced because new words and concepts are encountered in meaningful contexts. (Sealy, 2017)

The curriculum as a standards-based model

The National Curriculum is a blueprint for what any school is seeking to replicate in terms of the knowledge that pupils should have acquired during their time in their primary school. For some schools, notably academies, there is no prescription to follow the National Curriculum. However, the standards set out within it provide a useful starting point whatever the relevant ownership and status of the school. The National Curriculum created in 2013 ready for implementation in 2014 is what is known as a standards-based curriculum (Williams, 2013). It carefully sets out expectations of what pupils should know, understand and be able to do at certain points along their primary journey.

Assessment is the key driver to what is to be taught and what pupils will learn against end-of-year expectations. Effectively, these targets define when pupils are deemed to have mastered the concept, become unconsciously competent in their use of associated skills or demonstrated that they have retained knowledge that they can take forward to build new learning along the way. In the core programmes of study for maths, English and science the standards are carefully crafted to demonstrate how pupils will learn, layering their understanding year on year and across Key Stage 1, lower Key Stage 2 and then upper Key Stage 2. In order to plan a teaching sequence, all those planning and delivering the core curriculum must look at the continuum of learning from Year 1 to Year 6.

The mastery model usually involves teaching less content but to a greater depth. There are, however, issues with this model where mixed ability classes of anything up to 30 pupils are all working at their own pace, some understanding more than others, some unable to grasp even the basic concepts, and some where misconception may lead to problems in the future. It is, therefore, essential that teachers ask some basic questions as they grapple with the concept of mastery:

- When should the teacher move the majority of the class on to look at the next standard or deal with new knowledge, when some pupils in the class have clearly not understood?
- How does the teacher build strategies to support those pupils who have not mastered the specific learning task?
- Should there be opportunities for those who are quick to grasp the standard and exceed expectations to undertake more stretching and challenging tasks within the same topic or move on to more advanced standards before the rest of the class are ready to do so?

Building a consensus on the answers to the questions above and many others that might arise as primary teachers try to develop progressive strategies for ensuring pupils can meet the end-of-year expectations, is difficult for even the most exceptional subject specialist. Many primary teachers and their subject leads simply don't have the relevant knowledge and deep understanding of how to teach to these exacting standards never mind trying to differentiate the approach that will hopefully lead to all pupils achieving the expected end-of-year targets.

The changes that came into being with the new National Curriculum required a shift in the way teachers plan what to teach. The standards-based model requires them to carefully unpick the knowledge, understanding and skills that each subject demands and then decide on how to assess whether or not each pupil has met the standard. The standards in the core subjects, including science, clearly show the sequence of learning over time: each year is the springboard for the next year and the planned curriculum must incorporate how the teacher will assess whether or not the standard has been met and also whether the pupil is ready for the next stage of learning.

Below is a set of steps for those tasked with planning and delivering the curriculum that will help to create a consistent and cohesive approach where staff work together to build a consensus of what will be taught, to what depth and in what order. These are:

- Deciding what to teach linked to the subject content outlined in the programmes of study
- Defining the end-of-year expectation in terms of standards of achievement
- Developing differentiated materials either using the next-year standards or where some pupils are given further tasks that deepen their knowledge and understanding or that will provide extra help and guidance where mastery has not yet been achieved
- Lessons are planned taking account of the standards within the programmes of study
- There are opportunities for all pupils to have access to deep knowledge, concepts and skills that will support them in the quest for mastery of the standards
- Opportunities for retrieval practice and reinforcement of the learning are incorporated into the planning
- Assessment is an integral part of the planning process and formative assessment provides an opportunity to assess where pupils are along the journey towards mastery of the standards
- Attention is given to pace so that time is used to maximise the learning across all subjects within the National Curriculum

Understanding what is meant by a standards-based curriculum is an essential starting point for those with a responsibility for designing a curriculum that builds layers of learning over time and creates for pupils many opportunities to access the knowledge presented to them, to practise and strengthen their skill set and to understand the concepts that knit the knowledge together within the subject and across the rest of the curriculum. It is therefore essential that there is alignment across all subjects so that the same standards are applied in the context of the English, maths and science schemes of work as for all the other foundation subjects. This will not be easy for many primary teachers who do not have the subject expertise to determine the standards and age level expectations at the end of each year or key stage for the foundation subjects.

Table 6.1 draws together the aims and purpose of study that represents the current science curriculum for Key Stage 1 and 2. The science knowledge is explicit – how it is acquired is much more generic.

Table 6.1 Thinking and working scientifically – deepening knowledge, broadening understanding over time

Aims for thinking scientifically	Sequencing knowledge and conceptual understanding	The nature processes and methods of science
All pupils:- • Develop scientific knowledge and conceptual understanding through the specific disciplines of biology, chemistry and physics • Develop understanding of the nature, processes and methods of science through different types of science enquiries that help to answer scientific questions about the world around them • Are equipped with the scientific knowledge required to understand the uses and implications of science, today and for the future	• Secure understanding of each block of knowledge and concepts • Describe associated processes and key characteristics • Be familiar with and use technical terminology • Build up an extended specialist vocabulary • Apply mathematical knowledge • Collect, present and analyse data • Understand the social and economic implications of science in the wider school curriculum	• Scientific enquiry including, observing closely and over time • Pattern seeking • Identifying • Classifying and grouping • Comparative and fair testing • Research using secondary sources • Collecting, analysing and presenting data • Developing scientific vocabulary through articulating science concepts clearly and precisely • Using simple experiments • Performing simple tests • Compare and contrast

Taken from the Science Programme of Study for Key Stage 1 & 2 (DfE, 2014)

Studying the science programme of study carefully there is a very clear sequenced pathway towards what pupils should know and be able to do by the end of Year 6. There are also opportunities to reflect on the learning, revisit topics, themes and knowledge and reinforcement of the learning as an integral part of assessing how pupils are progressing, who is nearly there, who needs to be challenged and who needs extra support.

Early Years Foundation Stage – phonics and the building blocks of learning

The starting point must be the Early Years Foundation Stage (EYFS). It is here where children begin to formalise their learning experiences that start at birth or maybe even before. It is essential that all those who plan the curriculum in Key Stage 1 and 2 have a profound understanding of what children should know and be able to do by the end of this vital stage.

The EYFS Framework sets out three overarching principles (Early Years Foundation Stage (EYFS) statutory guidance, 2021)

- Learning and development
- Assessment
- Safeguarding and welfare

The framework states seven areas of learning (EYFS statutory guidance, 2021)

- Communication and language
- Personal, social and emotional development (PSED)
- Literacy
- Mathematics
- Understanding the world
- Expressive arts and design

A series of early learning goals defines what teachers are striving for in terms of achievement for children as they progress towards Year 1. Outlined below are some of the goals. It is not possible to reproduce them in their entirety here and there are many hooks for teachers who are planning for Year 1 learning to focus on to begin to plan the next steps in learning for pupils in Key Stage 1 and beyond.

So in a nutshell, some of the goals are set out here:

- Developing pupils' spoken language underpins all seven areas of development
- Personal, Social and Emotional Development (PSED) is crucial for children to lead healthy and happy lives
- Children learn to look after their bodies, make friends, co-operate and resolve conflict
- Children develop gross motor skills and fine motor control skills and precision as well as feedback from teachers
- Children develop a love of reading through language comprehension and word reading
- Children develop a strong grounding in number to develop the necessary building blocks to excel mathematically and develop positive and interest in mathematics
- Guiding children towards making sense of the world around them
- Developing children's artistic and cultural awareness to foster imagination and creativity

EYFS Framework (DfE, 2020)

Setting out the list above is a taster – the only way to build a true picture of the rich learning that takes place in early years is to read and digest the EYFS framework. Those with responsibility for the next stage in learning need to be familiar with the principles, the areas of learning and the early learning goals in order that they can ensure that the curriculum plan for Key Stage 1:

- Builds on the language and number skills children have so far developed
- Supports pupils to continue to develop confidence in themselves and in their ability to socialise
- Knows what has been taught that helps children to understand their place in the world
- Knows the kinds of opportunities they have had to be expressive through a growing cultural and artistic awareness

Understanding the critical importance of this stage in the education of the whole child cannot be underestimated. Where children have not experienced an opportunity to learn in a pre-school setting will set them apart from those who have. The issue of parental influence is also highly exposed in terms of confidence, competence and motivation to learn. Where pupils have parents who engage in conversation, who read to and with their children, who have books and other reading material at home and who enrich their child's experience within their own cultural landscape at home and in the wider community are already on their way in terms of how they will continue to learn in Key Stage 1 and for the rest of their time in education and in their life as adults. There are many pupils who do not have this advantage. Careful consideration and a profound understanding of the importance of learning in this first and crucial phase is the responsibility of primary school senior and curriculum leaders. Creating opportunities for pupils who will need nurture and an opportunity to experience some of the content of the EYFS framework needs to be balanced with content that builds on prior learning for those who have been through a positive pre-school experience.

Creating a consensus on how planning focuses on building on prior learning

The curriculum, although defined as individual subjects where each subject has distinct and clear standards that pupils must work towards, there are also many connections, concepts and skills that transcend individual subjects. The standards set out the essential knowledge, skills and understanding that pupils should achieve by the end of a given year or period of time. There is a distinct and defined sequential ladder where what is taught in one year dovetails into the next. There are connections and concepts that transcend individual subjects and skills that are essential to ensure pupils access knowledge and understanding across all the subjects. It is therefore not possible to create a seamless learning pathway unless there is a consensus and collaboration as to what and when certain standards and the depth to which they are taught are congruent so that the standards are aligned across all subjects, both core and foundation.

So, the primary curriculum needs to be mapped out at whole-school level and not by individual teachers. Units of work need to be defined and the pace of learning decided upon in weeks, half terms and terms. Teachers need to be an integral part of the planning as it is they who will be shaping the knowledge and deciding on the pedagogical approaches that will ensure pupils learn and deepen their understanding. They will also be the ones who will assess progress and achievement of the standards defined in the curriculum.

Where the curriculum is carefully structured in this way teachers can see what should have been taught in the previous year or the previous term and have a clear plan as to how what he or she will teach builds on prior learning and allows the pupils to deepen their knowledge and understanding. The teacher can use the learning from the previous year to ascertain what pupils have remembered, what they know and where there may be misconceptions. Recall and retrieval of knowledge will help pupils to remember their previous learning and reinforce how what they have learnt already is connected to their new learning.

Planning what will be taught requires subject and curriculum experts to use the tools that are readily available within the programmes of study in the pursuit of a deeper understanding of what is meant by sequencing. We know that the core knowledge in English, maths and science programmes of study are carefully sequenced from early years to Year 6. So that is a good starting point for knowing what to teach when in all three core subjects of English, maths and science. This creates a blueprint for planning the sequence necessary to ensure depth and breadth of sequencing in the foundation subjects.

Planning backwards – defining pupil achievement, progression and depth of understanding

Sequencing the curriculum in order to build a model of progression that allows pupils to layer their learning is a useful tactic so that those involved in the process know what they want pupils to have achieved by the time they leave the primary stage of their education.

This curriculum model requires an almost backward design (Griffith and Burns, 2014). Assessment of the learning is entwined within the decisions about what to teach and how to ensure pupils are deepening their learning. Teachers need to break down the relevant standards for each year and determine what to teach when. This approach provides teachers with an opportunity to look closely at the teaching sequence and build a learning pathway where pupils are deepening their understanding. Time is taken to ensure pupils can retain knowledge through conceptual understanding that does not overload the working memory and ensures that over time pupils retain powerful knowledge ready to tackle the next set of incremental standards.

There is no short cut to managing this approach to designing the curriculum. Long-term planning is a feature as is the need to ensure that all those involved are thoroughly grounded in an understanding of the standards to be achieved as part of a process that builds on prior learning and leads to clearly defined end points. There must be an alignment between what is planned at whole school level and what is taught in the classroom. This, inevitably, requires the collaboration of those with responsibility for the long-term whole-school plan and then how lesson sequences are planned at classroom level.

Everyone involved in developing this curriculum and assessment model will need access to continuing professional development and opportunities for ongoing learning conversations to establish consistency and evidence that the learning for pupils is sequential and will ensure that by the end of Year 6 all pupils have acquired depth and breadth of knowledge and achieved their full potential.

Aligning pedagogy and learning with curriculum standards

A simple diagram provides an understanding of the triangular process that defines the interrelationship between curriculum intent and implementation (Figure 6.1).

It will be highly beneficial for all those with responsibility for planning a sequential curriculum to look closely at the detailed and highly prescriptive programmes of study for English, maths and science.

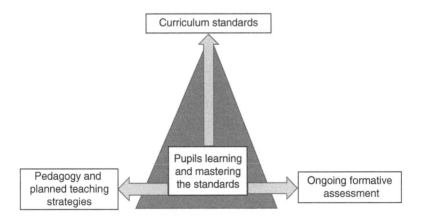

Figure 6.1 The sequence of learning in the core subjects

Adapted from Williams (2013).

For English the curriculum is broken down into Speaking and Listening, Reading, Writing and Spelling and Grammar. There is a clear and sequential narrative that provides the teacher with the opportunity to plan in incremental steps towards age-related expectations. Similarly in maths, the sequence is carefully laid out in terms of what will be taught in each year across a range of mathematical concepts including, number, measurement, geometry, statistics, area and ratio and proportion. The science curriculum is rich in detail and content across a range of interrelated scientific starting points.

A process of interpreting the standards and decoding what teachers are aiming to achieve is an important stage in implementing the core as it is laid down in the National Curriculum. This takes time and requires collaboration across the subject disciplines; there are, however, clear advantages of dedicating time to a deep dive into their construction and required outcomes. Working together means that teachers can share their own interpretation and agree on the key elements of learning that are essential to the development of a curriculum that will deliver success for all learners at key points along their learning journey. Teachers and their subject leads begin to develop a consensus of understanding that helps them to see how the different components of the curriculum combine to create rich content that is taught through innovative and creative pedagogy.

A further advantage of collective planning is to create opportunities for those who have limited subject knowledge to work with more experienced specialists. This approach also reduces the risk of creating a content-rich curriculum that does not challenge all pupils, where some teachers have low expectations of what pupils can achieve. So, joint planning creates the opportunity to unpick the standards into their key elements and components in order to establish what will be taught in relation to skills, knowledge and conceptual understanding. It is then possible to use this list to establish the teaching sequences that creates a ladder of progression that will ensure breadth and depth are an integral part of the process.

In terms of defining the end points from which to start to create a sequenced curriculum it is a good idea to start with the aims and purpose of study. These are generic to both Key Stage 1 and Key Stage 2 and so they are written to define what needs to be in place to ensure these aims are met by the end of Year 6. The purpose of study explains how English has a pre-eminent place in education and society. There is an emphasis on the importance of reading as the ultimate route to ensuring that pupils develop culturally, emotionally, intellectually, socially and spiritually. There should be a focus on literature and how it plays a significant part in developing the whole pupil. Essentially the purpose of study concludes that those who do not learn to speak, read and write fluently and confidently are effectively disenfranchised.

The National Curriculum for English aims to ensure that all pupils:

- Read easily, fluently and with good understanding
- Develop the habit of reading widely and often, for both pleasure and information
- Acquire a wide vocabulary, an understanding of grammar and knowledge of linguistic conventions for reading, writing and spoken language

- Appreciate our rich and varied literacy heritage
- Write clearly, accurately and coherently, adapting their language and style in and for a range of contexts, purposes and audiences
- Use discussions in order to learn: they should be able to elaborate and explain clearly their understanding and ideas
- Are competent in the arts of speaking and listening, making formal presentations, demonstrating to others and participating in debate

The sequence of learning in the core subjects of English and maths

In order to ensure that these aims can be met English subject leaders and teachers must look in detail as to what is being asked for in both the overarching aims and in how these are broken down as statements in the statutory requirements for each year from Year 1 to Year 6. The question is, at the end of Year 6, what is the teaching sequence that will mean that pupils can read easily, fluently and with good understanding, how wide is a wide vocabulary, what elements of our literary heritage are essential? What will constitute clear, accurate and coherent writing and what is the range of contexts, purposes and audiences we should be encouraging? How competent do we want pupils to be in the art of speaking and listening, making formal presentations and participating in debate?

In Key Stage 1 there is clear progression between what is expected to be covered in Year 1 and then in Year 2. For reading in Year 1 learning words through reading is essentially through the use of phonics to decode words and developing an understanding of common exception words. During Year 2, pupils must continue to apply phonics until they are automatically fluent, read accurately and quickly and continue to develop a bank of exception words that they can remember and use with accuracy. The progression is carefully defined from the beginning of Year 1 to the end of Year 2. The same applies to comprehension, where in Year 1 the emphasis is on developing pleasure in reading and motivation to read widely. There is also an emphasis on being familiar with stories they read and that are read to them. In Year 2 pupils should be encouraged to express views about a wide range of fiction along with a deeper focus on non-fiction. They should also begin to infer, make predictions and express their own opinions in discussion and debate. As far as writing is concerned, pupils in Year 1 should be developing sentences, sequencing those sentences and building short narratives. By the end of Year 2 they should be planning what they are going to write, writing more detailed narratives and beginning to evaluate and correct their own writing.

Planning for Key Stage 2 English does require that subject leaders and teachers have a profound understanding of what has been taught and learnt in Key Stage 1. The development of fluency in reading and competence in more detailed narrative writing as well as a growing ability to speak confidently, make presentations, listen well, and ask and answer questions should already be quite well developed. There is a desire for all pupils to achieve the age-related grade level standards at the end of each key stage. This is most unlikely for all pupils. Those with responsibility for the curriculum development in Key Stage 2 must have and communicate data about the competence and level of ability each pupil has achieved as part of formative assessment that continues over the whole key stage process. Low-stakes summative assessment of ability and level of competence will also help to assess who has and who has not yet achieved age-related expectations.

In the maths programmes of study the same overarching principles apply. The first place to go is to the aims for the whole programme which are simply stated – pupils should be fluent in the fundamentals of mathematics, reason mathematically and solve problems through the application of mathematics.

The standards within the programmes of study are carefully structured to allow for systematic teaching. There is an emphasis to actively develop mathematical language, pace their learning with regular opportunities to rehearse, recall, refresh, refine, read, reason and build on prior learning. The standards are carefully constructed to move the pupil towards identifiable points of assessment. Assessment of the learning is a key component of the planning so that the teacher can establish who has mastered the standards and who needs more scaffolding or support to move them closer to mastery.

Deepening knowledge and understanding in science over time

The emphasis on the purpose of a science education in the primary phase has changed since the introduction of the new curriculum in 2014. Instead of 'How Science Works' the emphasis is on 'Thinking and Working Scientifically'. This requires some thought for whoever is responsible for planning and overseeing the implementation of primary science. Thinking scientifically suggests that before the teacher can support pupils towards being able to think scientifically, they themselves need to do the same. Simply focusing on creating opportunities for pupils to see how water is absorbed by a sponge or how light makes a rainbow is not enough. The standards within the programmes of study require a sequence that deepens understanding over time. Science follows the same progressive language as for English and maths and lays out clearly sequenced learning requiring pupils as early as Year 1 to identify, compare, observe, recognise and explore. This requires much more than simply introducing the potential for understanding what different materials are used for in a variety of everyday situations. Pupils need to group together materials with different properties, make comparisons and observe how some materials change shape. They must also distinguish between an object and the material from which it is made.

There is a clear sequence that provides benchmarks for what pupils should know and be able to do at the end of each year. This provides the opportunity for the planning of units that carefully define what will be assessed in relation to the standards, how to create time for recall and retrieval to re-enforce the learning and how to identify where pupils have gaps in their learning or where misconceptions have led to barriers to learning.

A planning grid can draw the elements of a sequenced curriculum together using the standards that are defined in the core programmes of study. Table 6.2 shows a simple example taken from Year 4 science.

Table 6.2 Some elements of a sequenced curriculum for science

Standards	Benchmarks for learning	Pedagogy and learning
Compare and group materials together, according to whether they are solids, liquids or gases Observe that some materials change state when they are heated or cooled and measure the temperature at which this happens in degrees Celsius Identify the part played by evaporation and condensation in the water cycle and associate the rate of evaporation with temperature	Identify solids and liquids Know that there are liquids other than water Know that liquids do not change in volume when they are poured into different containers The same material can exist as both solid and liquid Liquids can change to a solid and solids to liquids Understanding the term evaporation and what happens when a liquid evaporates Explore examples of evaporation such as drying Understanding the term condensation Know about air and how it contains water vapour Know about the word and concept of temperature Understand about water in relation to the weather and geographical features	Asking relevant questions Setting up simple, practical enquiries and comparative tests Measuring accurately using standard units and a range of equipment Gather, record and classify data and present data in a variety of ways Record findings using simple scientific language and representations such as diagrams, drawings or graphs Encouraging oral reporting of findings and writing up findings Use results to draw simple conclusions and suggest improvements, make predictions and ask questions Identify differences, similarities or changes related to simple scientific ideas

(Phrases taken from the Year 4 science programme of study, DfE, 2014)

Developing a consensus on sequencing in the foundation subjects

If there is a clear and well-defined sequencing of the core subjects, carefully crafted to give schools a clear and well-mapped pathway to follow, it makes sense to use the same approach when focusing on how to ensure a knowledge-rich curriculum can be delivered for the foundation subjects as well.

There are two key elements that must be established in order that real strength exists in building a consensus on what should be taught, to what depth and in what order. Firstly, just as for the core subjects that have been carefully constructed, the key is to start with what it is we want our pupils to achieve by the end of their time in primary school, planning backwards from what will be assessed to ascertaining what will be taught in relation to subject matter. Secondly, how the knowledge will be taught to ensure pupils are developing a range of skills for learning can make conceptual connections and can apply their learning in a variety of contexts that relate to both the core subjects and other foundation subjects.

Each of the foundation subjects is set out in the same way:

- **The purpose of study** explains what is expected that will provide pupils with a high-quality education to deepen their subject knowledge and give them subject-specific skills in order to access and retain their growing understanding
- **The aims for each subject** constitutes a set of overarching aims for both Key Stage 1 and 2 that define what pupils should know and can do by the end of their time in primary school
- **Attainment targets** explain that by the end of each key stage, pupils are expected to know, apply and understand the matters, skills and processes specified in the relevant programme of study
- **The subject content** for the foundation subjects is divided into Key Stage 1 content and Key Stage 2 content. There is a sequence to the knowledge that pupils are expected to acquire

For example, let's take the history programme of study. The purpose of study explains that a high-quality history education will help pupils gain a coherent knowledge and understanding of the past and a curiosity to know more. Pupils should be taught to ask perceptive questions, think critically, weigh evidence, sift arguments and develop perspective and judgement. They must learn about the complexity of people's lives, the process of change, the diversity of societies and relationships between different groups, as well as considering their own identity and the challenges of their time.

The aims for all the foundation subjects provide a sequenced key to how the statutory subject matter is taught to ensure pupils gain deep and specific subject perspective. In history for instance the aims are to build a coherent, chronological narrative of the UK and the wider world; understand abstract terms and historical concepts, know about methods of historical enquiry and to gain historical perspective. (a precis of a detailed bulleted list of aims taken from the Key Stage 2 programme of study for history).

It is the subject content that helps to clarify some of the processes and methods that teachers might use to create for pupils a sequenced deepening of knowledge and understanding. These are broken down for Key Stage 1 and 2 and provide a sequence that does require some careful planning. Once again, let us take history as an example (see Table 6.3).

Table 6.3 Examples of the breadth and depth of sequencing the learning in Key Stage 1 and into Key Stage 2

Key Stage 1	Key Stage 2
Use common words and phrases about their growing awareness of the passing of time	Establish clear narratives within and across periods of study
Be able to describe similarities and differences	Note connections, contrasts and trends
Use a wide vocabulary	Use appropriate historical terms
Ask and answer questions	Devise historically valid questions about, change, cause, similarities and differences and significance
Understand key features of events	
Know the different ways we find out about the past	
Know how the past is represented in different ways	Construct informed responses through thoughtful selection and organisation of relevant historical information
Continue to chronologically secure knowledge and understanding of the past	Understand how our knowledge of the past is constructed from a range of sources

Phrases taken from the history programme of study for Key Stage 1 and 2 DfE (2014)

The complexity and depth that is revealed within these short documents that make up the programmes of study for the foundation subjects need to be an essential tool in planning how to teach and in determining what to teach, to what depth and ultimately to know what to assess.

For subject leads and their teams, a focus on the processes and methods by which pupils can access subject-specific knowledge and understanding gives them an opportunity to then dovetail what they will teach in their subject with what is being taught in the core subjects. The example of history above reveals the reliance on the use of English skills to support the increasing development of historical understanding: use common words and phrases, describe similarities and differences, read sources of evidence, devise questions, construct informed responses, establish a clear narrative. The opportunity to reinforce the development of oracy skills, reading widely and learning how to write fluently and extensively over time, are there in abundance. There may also be opportunities to reinforce numeracy skills as well – the chronology of time, Roman numerals, BC and AD and so on. Science and history also cross paths – the history of medicine, the story of certain inventors and other famous people, famous discoveries and changes in transport, technology or sanitation. It is also prudent to mention that many of the other foundation subjects share similar themes and concepts.

The more opportunities there are for pupils to make connections, recall core learning as part of their foundation learning and deepen their skills in both literacy and numeracy within their foundation learning the greater the opportunity for pupils to exercise their working memory, reinforce their understanding and retain their learning within their long-term memory and ensure it stays there into their next stage of learning and possibly forever (Lemov, 2010).

The uniqueness of learners – the concept of mastery in a mixed-ability reality

The primary years are a critical time for learning. However, it is not a level playing field for all pupils. The earlier we focus on making sure all our pupils can grasp the basics and are exposed to a rich and challenging curriculum the more likely those pupils who come from more disadvantaged starting points can achieve the same in the longer term as their more advantaged peers. The sooner the absolute goal is set to ensure all pupils achieve mastery of each element of their learning across the curriculum means that there is less opportunity for pupils to be left behind. Being certain that all pupils can achieve with good teaching and a positive mindset is the first step in creating a culture of self-belief that permeates throughout a school and all the learners within it.

This diagram is adapted from a similar diagram that focuses on mastery in maths (My interpretation of the original diagram published by (Drury 2015)). Here, the emphasis is on the message that the principles apply to any subject. It is the opportunity to provide pupils with specific problems to solve that can create opportunities for them to explore the concepts that underpin the learning. Effective and expert pedagogy supports the use of language pertinent to the subject and demonstrates pupils'

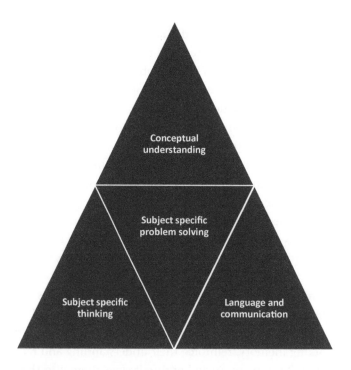

Figure 6.2 The components that lead to mastery learning within the foundation subjects.

Adapted from Drury (2015). © Oxford University Press 2015. Reproduced with permission of the Licensor through PLSclear.

growing knowledge within a subject area. Within this approach there are clear opportunities for pupils to show their growing ability to use a range of skills, vocabulary and subject-specific thinking to celebrate their depth of knowledge and understanding.

E. D. Hirsch, in his book *Cultural Literacy*, echoes the point. He asks the question, 'Why have we failed to give (pupils) the information they lack?' His answer:

> Chiefly, because of educational formalism, which encourages us to ignore the fact that identifying and imparting the information a child is missing is most important in the earliest stages, when the task is most manageable. At age six, when a child must acquire knowledge critical for continuing development the total quantity of missing information is not huge. (Hirsch, 1988: 111)

Focusing on a mastery model creates the foundations that will provide the evidence and the process that ensure learning is sequenced over time and leads to all pupils accessing and achieving the age-related expectations that are contained within and across all curriculum subjects. A mastery model is cumulative and requires pupils to master basic skills or concepts before moving on to the next steps in learning. In this model it is expected that teachers plan to take longer with teaching new content and ensuring all pupils have grasped the concept before moving on to the next topic. It also requires that all pupils, even those that find maths or indeed any subject difficult, access all the key concepts and skills. Higher achieving pupils have access to opportunities to deepen their learning of the same concepts and skills and are not exposed to more content that moves them on to the next steps too quickly. This approach helps lower attainers to keep up and allows higher achievers to gain a much deeper foundation in key concepts and skills. All of this is part of crucial planning and ongoing professional development for teachers and subject leaders to ensure that they understand the principles, have the pedagogy to deliver a differentiated but deep learning experience for all pupils and build a consistent assessment process that provides the benchmarks and assurances that all pupils are making progress.

Teachers need to work together to plan a sequence of learning linked to the standards that pupils need to master. The aim of a mastery model is depth of learning rather than simply coverage of the content. Where pupils deeply understand the basic concepts of a subject they have the foundations to learn new content over time. Mastery is usually the domain of the maths curriculum but the principles apply across all subjects. Sequencing the learning over time is an essential element of the mastery approach to learning. Spending time to master the basic concepts and understanding the fundamental purpose as to why this is important creates the sequence that then builds on these well-taught and understood basic starting points.

A mastery model requires teachers to focus on differentiation for depth of knowledge. They need to know what this means and how to plan for the accumulation of knowledge over time, with reference to reflection, retrieval and practice to exercise the working memory as well as helping pupils to make connections with prior learning within and across subjects that leads to depth of learning that sticks.

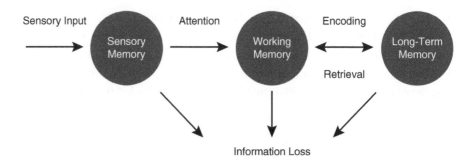

Figure 6.3 Paying attention to cognitive science and its fundamental importance in understanding memory and the retention of knowledge

Adapted from Education Endowment Foundation (2021)

Understanding cognitive science and the power of memory on learning is an essential element of learning for the new and seasoned teachers (EEF, 2021). A mastery model focuses on putting cognitive science into practice. Building a deep understanding of how to rehearse, recall, refresh, refine, read and reason as part of planning and implementing the curriculum across the core and the foundation subjects is a good starting point. The four components in the bullets here should be an integral part of the planning and implementation process.

- Conceptual understanding
- Sequencing and cross-curricular connections
- Subject-specific thinking
- Deepening understanding

Sequencing and the taxonomies that define progression and learning

This chapter establishes that there is a sequence to the way the curriculum should be taught. The English, maths and science curriculum are clearly set out year by year. This is not the case in the foundation programmes of study but the language and processes within the core subjects do provide a means of mapping how and when to support pupils to extend their thinking and demonstrate their deeper understanding over time using their literacy and numeracy skills and growing ability to think and work scientifically.

In science in Year 1 pupils must *identify, describe, compare, associate and find out how*; this continues into Year 2 but pupils then must also demonstrate that they can *explore and compare*. By Year 6 pupils are expected to do all the above as well as *report and present findings, use abstract ideas to explain phenomena, use simple models and identify scientific evidence*. The move from the more simple describe, recall and explain to analysis, justification and evaluation, of course, links directly to the language of the assessment criteria that determines the mark schemes for the National Qualification Framework and prepares primary school pupils for a secondary journey towards being ready for GCSE and beyond. The curriculum and the knowledge it holds within it across all subjects, as a part of conceptual learning and as a receptor for the skills pupils need to access, is a continuum. Constructing the curriculum journey is essentially collaborative where all teachers know the part they play in ensuring all pupils arrive at the end of each year and each key stage achieving their absolute full potential.

Conclusion

Delve into the National Curriculum programmes of study and there is no doubt that there is a clear and structured sequence to the knowledge pupils are expected to learn over their time in the primary phase. This is very carefully constructed in the core subjects of English and maths and also in the science curriculum. Within all three there are also opportunities for pupils to recall and revisit certain elements of their learning before being introduced to new information and knowledge. The language of progression is also evident and provides opportunities to introduce challenge to extend understanding and deepen knowledge acquisition. There is far less prescription in the foundation subjects, but the aims and processes provide sufficient scope to build deep and rich sequential learning opportunities for all pupils to have access to the broadest curriculum offer.

The knowledge, the concepts and the skills are intertwined within all subjects and create a wealth of opportunity for pupils to see and make connections, deepen their understanding and make progress towards achieving the standards within the core and across all of the foundation subjects. The key to unlocking profound and sequential learning is to create the time for collaborative planning so that there is a clear map of what will be taught when, and how pupils will build on prior learning and master the skills required to acquire deep knowledge and understanding.

─────────────────────── Top tips ───────────────────────

- All teachers work together to establish their understanding of how to deliver a standards-based curriculum
- Work out a consistent whole-school strategy that ensures differentiation provides all pupils with the same opportunity to access depth and breadth across all subjects
- Planning what and how to teach the foundation subjects should take into account where there are clear connections to what pupils are learning in the core subjects

- Create regular opportunities for retrieval and reinforcement in order to ensure pupils are building on prior learning
- Teachers should look in detail at the aims and purposes of study and methods as well as the subject content
- All subject leads and teachers should have access to and look closely at the Statutory Early Years Framework and take account of the essential building blocks of learning that should be in place as well as assessing where they are not
- The curriculum should be mapped out at whole-school level with the involvement of subject leads and teachers and regularly reviewed as part of a collective quality assurance process
- The key to success is to plan backwards, focusing on what pupils should know and can do by the end of a year, a key stage or their time in primary school
- There must be clear alignment with what is planned at whole-school level and what is taught in the classroom
- Continuing professional development and positive conversations about how the curriculum is planned and delivered will deliver a consistent message that the curriculum vision is indeed implemented successfully

References

Department for Education (DfE) (2014) *National Curriculum in England: Framework for Key Stages 1 and 2*. London: DfE.

Department for Education (DfE) (2021) *Statutory Framework for the Early Years Foundation Stage*. (EYFS) London: DfE.

Drury, H. (2015) *Mastering Mathematics: Teaching to Transform Achievement*. Oxford: Oxford University Press.

Education Endowment Foundation (2021) *Cognitive Science Approaches in the Classroom*. London: Education Endowment Foundation.

Griffith, A. and Burns, M. (2014) *Outstanding Teaching: Teaching Backwards*. Carmarthen: Crown House.

Hirsch, E. D. (1988) *Cultural Literacy: What Every American Needs to Know*. New York: Vintage Books.

Lemov, D. (2010) *Teach Like a Champion: 49 Techniques that Put Students on the Path to College*. San Francisco: Jossey-Bass.

Sealy, C. (2017) 'The 3D Curriculum that Promotes Remembering', *Primarytimerydotcom*. 28 October 2017 [Blog]. Available at: https://primarytimery.com/2017/10/28/the-3d-curriculum-that-promotes-remembering/ (accessed 27 July 2022).

Williams, J. C. (2013) *Towards a Standards-Based Curriculum: A Toolkit for the New Primary Curriculum in England*. London: Publish Nation.

7

ASSESSING LEARNING: CREATING A COLLABORATIVE AND COHESIVE STRATEGY FOR POSITIVE FORMATIVE ASSESSMENT

The dialogue between pupils and a teacher should be thoughtful, reflective, focused to evoke and explore understanding, and conducted so that all pupils have an opportunity to think and to express their ideas. (Black and Wiliam, 1998)

Assessment and the curriculum

To be genuinely praised for getting it right is comforting for every learner wherever they are on their learning journey and it is the experience of most primary teachers, including myself, that pupils want to achieve what is asked of them. In this chapter I am focusing on much more than just the tick in the book, the written comment at the end of a piece of extended writing, the comments in the margin or the grade or mark that defines where pupils are along the bell curve or flight path of achievement.

Assessment is one of the most profound pedagogies in a teacher's repertoire. Assessment should be an integral part of planning for every topic. Planning backwards from what is expected pupils will achieve at the end of a series of lessons, at the end of a topic and at the end of a year or a key stage is the key to making sure that the planned content will secure a deepening of understanding, the layering of increasingly complex knowledge and the ability for all pupils to use their skills to access that knowledge and demonstrate their growing understanding. In order to make this happen all teachers and their line managers must see the bigger picture in relation to the age-related standards that seek to ensure pupils have achieved their full potential by the time they leave primary school.

The emergence of the new curriculum in 2014 for most schools in England and the subsequent far-reaching changes to the Ofsted (2022) framework requires a singular change in the way all schools reframe their approach to assessment and focus not on data but on powerful strategies for learning conversations and opportunities for teachers to know each and every one of their pupils and what they believe they are capable of achieving.

The previous three chapters look in detail at the skills, knowledge and concepts pupils need to master on their curriculum journey and how the learning is sequenced over time to ensure pupils deepen their knowledge and progress well towards clearly defined end points, whatever those are and wherever they are defined. In order for teachers to plan assessment of the learning it is essential that they have a profoundly deep understanding of the standards they want their pupils to achieve.

This chapter focuses on the imperative to ensure that assessment is an integral part of the process of planning a broad and balanced curriculum offer that leads to deep learning of conceptual and factual knowledge and a clear understanding of the skills pupils must become competent in using in order that they can access the knowledge, facts and concepts and begin to manipulate their own thinking in order to use the higher-order taxonomies of explanation, analysis, synthesis and evaluation.

Assessment is therefore a mechanism for evaluating not only the quality of learning but also the effectiveness of pedagogy or teaching strategies that allow that learning to take place. Creating a cohesive and collaborative approach to assessment is CPD in action and all those involved will gain from the opportunity to be an integral part of understanding how formative assessment is an ongoing process and is vital to learning.

We are therefore rethinking the purpose of assessment where the process is an integral part of the business of teaching and learning.

So, there is a shift:

- From assessing to learn what pupils do not know to assessing to learn what pupils understand
- From using results to calculate grades to using results to inform next steps
- From end-of-term assessments by teachers to learners engaged in ongoing assessment of their work and the work of others
- From judgemental feedback that may harm pupil motivation to descriptive feedback that empowers and motivates learners to want to improve and learn more

Summative and formative assessment

To develop this theme further we must be clear as to the distinction between formative and summative assessment. The current accountability system, especially when 'high stakes' tests or examinations drive curriculum decisions, can mean that the focus is most definitely on 'teaching to the test' where the use of external test structures defines the what in terms of subject content and the how in terms of assessment of the learning of that content. This is, essentially, summative in nature and the outcome is to test whether the pupil has remembered enough to answer pre-determined questions. These kinds of tests often take place at the end of a sequence of learning and therefore there is no time for or opportunity to analyse the results and decide how to fill any gaps in knowledge, unpick misconceptions or try a different approach if it is clear that there is a distinct lack of understanding.

There is a place for testing. Pupils like tests, adults like tests, the popularity of games shows and quizzes on television certainly reinforces that assertion. Testing at points along the way to learning can provide the teacher with a window onto what pupils know, misconstrue and don't know. 'Low stakes' tests that are not subject to quantitative data constraints and that provide the teacher with the information to plan next steps in learning can be very beneficial.

Formative assessment is what happens in the classroom on a daily basis. It is the process whereby teachers are continually assessing how well pupils listen, absorb knowledge and become increasingly competent in the use of the skills they need to learn and progress. It is assessment of the learning that is taking place through observations that pupils are developing higher levels of response that allow them to become more curious, more analytical, begin to make connections, work together in groups and with their peers and build their own strategies for self-belief.

Table 7.1 shows different approaches to formative assessment that can contribute to learning.

Dylan Wiliam, one of the foremost protagonists of formative assessment (something he first called assessment for learning), suggests the following principles (Wiliam, 2011).

- Activating learning as instructional resources for one another
- Activating learners as owners of their own learning
- Clarifying, sharing and understanding the learning intention and criteria for success
- Providing feedback that moves learning forward
- Engineering effective classroom discussion, activities and learning tasks that elicit evidence of learning

The voices raised for the very essence of creating the culture where formative assessment or 'responsive teaching' create a classroom that vividly represents progressive and tangible learning is echoed by Ofsted (2022). Assessment, Ofsted says, should be an integral part of the planning process in relation to the curriculum and what we want pupils to know, learn and remember. It then becomes a natural pedagogy that supports learning and progression all the way through the implementation process and involves the learner in the process of evaluating their own learning and progress.

> Inspectors are looking to see that a school's assessment system supports the pupils' journeys through the curriculum. (Harford, 2018).

The Black Box that Black and Wiliam refer to (1998) could be an analogy to the flight box on an aeroplane. When opened it reveals the secrets of what goes on inside the classroom and maybe, similar to its use in aviation, what has gone wrong. However pernicious most teachers see lesson observation, the majority of their working lives

Table 7.1 Different approaches to formative assessment

• Where learners assess together in pairs	• Using quizzes and tests
• Comment only marking without grading	• Using red, amber green as tool to assess whether pupils have understood
• Sharing targets, learning objectives and success criteria	• Using higher order questioning to aid progression
• Using open questions to ensure pupils are challenged	• Feeding forward to encourage next steps in learning
• Focusing on reading and ensuring pupils comprehend what they are reading	• Using exemplars of different levels of response
• Listening to pupils talk about their learning	• Grading work with pupils

are spent with their pupils unobserved except perhaps by a member of a support team. Their excellent practice goes unnoticed as does their experimentation, their successes and frustrations, times when things don't work and times when weariness or high winds mean the planned lesson is abandoned and something simpler and easier to control takes over. Wiliam and Black look at assessment as the key to reflective practice where a continuous process of assessing pupil progress, looking for misconception and creating opportunities for recall and review all build a picture for the teacher of how their pedagogy, the resources they use and the opportunities they provide for pupils to create evidence of their growing understanding come together to create a culture of learning, encouragement and challenge.

The key messages that should be at the heart of developing a policy for formative assessment across the whole school are:

- Formative assessment is part of all learning and informs lesson planning, teaching strategies and assessment techniques
- There is a continued focus on standards that emphasise a continuum of learning from early years to post-16 and beyond
- There is an emphasis on mapping the curriculum across all phases to build a continuity and support transition
- There is a sharp focus on ensuring literacy and numeracy are integral to all learning
- There is an expectation that differentiation is achieved by emphasising deep knowledge through individual support and intervention that leads to mastery

The importance of cognitive science in the pursuit of knowledge

The theories surrounding an understanding of memory and how we create the right conditions for learning to take place are within the realm of cognitive science. Interestingly, I have no memory of ever learning about cognitive science when I trained as a teacher but that was a long time ago. It is now firmly entrenched within the Ofsted framework and therefore one would hope that trainee teachers are exposed to the vital messages that an understanding of working memory, cognitive load theory and the necessary steps to supporting pupils to ensure the information and knowledge finally arrives in the long-term memory are part of their learning.

Daisy Christodoulou in her book *Making Good Progress* considers the importance of the right form of formative assessment that leads to depth and breadth in learning. She says that formative assessment should be about identifying consequences so that what the teacher learns about the pupil's ability to understand and absorb the learning informs what the teacher plans and does next (Christodoulou, 2016).

Her list of essential features of effective formative assessment clearly focuses on the teacher having an understanding of cognitive science. She says formative assessment should be:

- Specific: focused on quite narrow content domains so that precise gaps can be identified for future teaching and further practice
- Frequent: building on the idea of regular retrieval practice to develop long-term memory and recall taken from cognitive science
- Repetitive: to ensure skills and retrieval are actually practised in a focused manner
- Recorded as raw marks to ensure the information is kept as close to the details of the original assessment without being morphed into a bell curved graph or standardised score

(Christodoulou, 2016)

In order to practically use an understanding of cognitive science in the decisions about what to assess and how to assess in a formative capacity, the teacher and all those who influence curriculum design and delivery must ask themselves the question 'What is learning?' Without an answer how do we know whether pupils have retained, understood and connected learning in a range of subjects and contexts. This is not an easy question. I like this definition taken from a paper called *Effective Learning* produced by the Institute of Education in 2002. It is referenced in Abbot (1994):

Learning ... That reflective activity which enables the learner to draw upon previous experience to understand and evaluate the present, so as to shape future action and formulate new knowledge.

The importance of prior learning is highlighted in the quote and suggests that new learning is enhanced as a result of what has already been taught. In order to accommodate and assimilate new ideas the pupil must have the opportunity to recall previous learning. In this way the teacher's role is to be adept at providing opportunities for pupils to recall, repeat, reflect and review and constantly building new knowledge that is woven into existing knowledge. Throughout this it is essential that the teacher and those involved in the process of planning and delivering the curriculum start with what the learning will lead to in terms of end points where the age-related standards benchmark how successful the process has been.

Each individual pupil has a capacity for learning but their ability to concentrate, build on their previous experiences and feel motivated with the subject matter all play their part in making it difficult to judge whether pupils have grasped a concept, understood a model, learnt important facts or deepened their understanding over time.

In relation to the assessment process, especially in terms of formative, ongoing and reflective assessment a simple model to use to focus on what is involved in learning is the one devised by Kolb (1984). He visualises learning as cyclical, where he describes the four elements in a learning process (Figure 7.1).

In order to learn there is activity that leads to the learner reading, writing, listening, drawing, discussing, painting, measuring, calculating or any number of other activities that can support some kind of opportunity for learning. Doing something

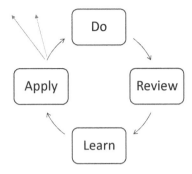

Figure 7.1 The process of deep learning adapted from Kolb

is not enough and in order to deepen their understanding there needs to be a process of reflection, how well, how successfully, how deeply, how confidently, with what help, what's next, what else, and so build on the capacity to think more deeply about the learning process and how much each pupil is actually learning. So we can then assume that learning has taken place in some meaningful way. However, in order to consolidate that learning there must be opportunities to apply the learning in a variety of different contexts. It is through this application that the teacher can assess a pupil's depth of understanding and what else he or she may need in terms of support so that any gaps in learning can be rectified or where challenge is required to take the learner beyond an undesirable comfort zone.

Curriculum cohesion within and across core and foundation subjects

Planning the curriculum requires collaboration so that there is a clear sequence of learning from early years to Year 6 that defines what will be taught in relation to concepts, skills and knowledge. Where teachers work in isolation in year groups or subject silos their understanding of what pupils are learning is limited – they cannot build on prior learning or help pupils towards mastery of their learning if they cannot assess their deepening understanding.

It takes time to create the space where those with responsibility for the curriculum can work together to create a tapestry of learning that defines age-related expectations and builds a picture shaped by a weft of knowledge, threads of developing skills and a fabric of reflection and recall over time. Where time is given to a collective and cogent overview of what will be taught and when from year to year, within subjects and in building cross-curricular cohesion, the benefits are profound.

The core learning within English and maths is carefully sequenced as discussed in Chapter 6. Science is equally detailed in how it is set out across Key Stage 1 and

Key Stage 2 within the National Curriculum programmes of study. So, this is a good place to start in relation to focusing on what to teach linked to the statutory requirements of content. However, focusing simply on this will not deliver the breadth and depth that leads to the acquisition of subject and conceptual knowledge and understanding over time.

Creating an assessment strategy for progression must include:

- Desirable and relevant learning aims
- Curriculum content linked to the standards
- Tasks and activities that lead to deep learning
- Creating the time to involve all pupils in the process of assessment
- Observations and feedback that reflect on pedagogy and practice in relation to how well pupils are learning
- Planning for challenge or 'desirable difficulties' Bjork (1994) that will stretch learners' potential
- Opportunities for continuous professional dialogue and decisions about pupils and progress with clear evidence that teachers know their pupils as individuals
- An ongoing process of evaluation and review that builds a culture of continuous professional learning

Why planning and assessing the curriculum should be in synergy with each other

The best practice is where there is a clear determination of senior leaders to create time for teams to work together to decide on the assessment methodology that emerges because of the choice of subject content, the standards pupils are expected to achieve at the end of each age-related stage and the quality of work produced. A team approach provides groups of teachers with the opportunity to work together to determine the teaching sequence, the conceptual understanding within and beyond subjects and the skills pupils will need to develop and become unconsciously competent at using.

Teams working within subject groups, across a phase or key stage, building their wider knowledge of the core and how this relates to other foundation learning, can learn from each other and begin to weave together a learning journey that makes sure all pupils have a rich vein of knowledge and understanding that leads to positive outcomes and strong evidence of learning. So, in preparing and planning curriculum content, those involved need to ask these questions:

- What are we assessing?
- How are we assessing?
- What impact does assessment have on learning?

The what, the how and the why of assessment

Let us look at the questions in Figure 7.2.

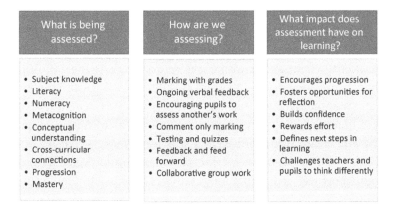

What is being assessed?	How are we assessing?	What impact does assessment have on learning?
• Subject knowledge • Literacy • Numeracy • Metacognition • Conceptual understanding • Cross-curricular connections • Progression • Mastery	• Marking with grades • Ongoing verbal feedback • Encouraging pupils to assess another's work • Comment only marking • Testing and quizzes • Feedback and feed forward • Collaborative group work	• Encourages progression • Fosters opportunities for reflection • Builds confidence • Rewards effort • Defines next steps in learning • Challenges teachers and pupils to think differently

Figure 7.2   Creating a structured approach to reflective and formative assessment

Looking in some detail at each of the above questions will build for subject teams and curriculum leaders a consistent and whole-school strategy that can be a framework that all teachers use as a basis for cohesive and progressive ongoing formative assessment. Creating an opportunity for collaborative planning highlights for those involved, the complexity of the curriculum, the way the standards are written and how teachers interpret them in order to create sequential learning from early years to Year 6.

What are we assessing?

The first premise here is to focus on what has been planned in terms of subject content and how it will be taught. The statutory requirements are clearly defined but do not in any way provide any guidance on how the subject matter should be taught and in what detail or complexity. It is to the aims, processes and purpose of study that planners and teachers of the curriculum should focus to determine their strategy for creating a sequential model that will help pupils to build on their prior learning, develop complexity in terms of deepening understanding and learn through problem-solving and enquiry.

In both English and maths, the sequence of learning is clearly laid out. What pupils learn in Year 1 is built upon in Year 2 and so on throughout Key Stage 1 and 2. There are also clear points along the way where teachers can revisit previous learning as part of a continuous model of learning to ensure that pupils have learnt the principles or to reassess how to reinforce the learning for those pupils who have not yet understood. An assessment plan should align with the standards set out for each year.

In order to create the plans that will establish what will be taught and therefore what will be assessed, teams need to focus on the key vocabulary that must form part of the teaching and learning. For instance, actively seeking out and planning how mathematical language is understood and used by pupils as they progress through the curriculum. In Year 1 it is crucial that the benchmarks which are the standards are used to assess how well pupils master the principles at the beginning of their learning journey. For each of the next five years up to Year 6 planning must put the standards at the forefront of teaching and assessment from unit to unit. There must be a relentless focus on learning, progress and mastery of skills, knowledge and understanding.

Creating an overarching plan that uses the standards as benchmarks provides a clearly defined blueprint for each year group to follow which will, by design, build on prior learning and create a fluid and highly structured process that leads to progression for all. In short, there is much greater transparency and clarity in terms of what is being taught, how well it is being taught and most crucially how well pupils are learning.

It is important that the planning of an assessment strategy also encompasses the use of English and maths in science and all of the other foundation subjects. Deepening the skills of reading, writing and oracy happen in every subject and recognising where the English and maths curriculum can be reinforced in other subject areas deepens competence and builds for pupils the opportunity to develop a rich vein of cross-curricular vocabulary through extensive reading of non-fiction, a greater depth in terms of quality of writing and real opportunities to make connections through debate and discussion within and across subject divides.

As we have seen previously, it is the core subjects – including science – that we can draw on to begin to develop a taxonomy that can be used across the whole spectrum of subjects. So, as an example, the science curriculum for Year 4 in relation to the content standards follows a pattern that asks pupils to identify, construct, recognise, compare, understand, give reasons, demonstrate and explain.

The history curriculum, for instance, although I could use an example from any of the foundation subjects, has in the aims section of the programme of study the following: know and understand, gain and deploy, know the methods, gain historical perspective, understand the passage of time. Once again the essential ingredient in creating a progressive model where all teachers can assess how well pupils are progressing is in dialogue. What exactly are we looking for from the work of a pupil who demonstrates that he or she has gained an understanding of historical perspective? What level of detail are we looking for when a Year 1 pupil gives a reason for why there is a change in a substance when it is heated or when a Year 4 pupil can articulate that some materials are better conductors than others?

Within the umbrella of focusing on what to assess, it is also for the teacher to create opportunities for pupils to think about how they are learning, how pupils learn together in groups or in peer-to-peer conversations, how well they listen, take notes and organise their own learning. Learning should be about awe and wonder where the pupil owns their own journey towards an awakening of the possibilities of knowledge (Didau, 2016). The Education Endowment Foundation's work on metacognition provides a wonderful insight into seven pillars of metacognition, a must for any teacher in search of inspiration linked to thinking and learning (EEF, 2018). Where the teacher encourages pupils to continually assess themselves, the ways in which they learn best and the bits of learning that interest them most, the possibilities for higher achievement and breadth and depth of progressive learning are limitless.

Finally in the pursuit of what to assess we need to focus on challenge. The work of Robert Bjork and his phrase 'desirable difficulties' (1994) captures the imagination for any teacher wanting to make sure that all pupils retain what he or she has taught them and ensure they are ready for more and will continually learn and be able to retrieve that learning. Using Bjork's theory (1994) by introducing ways to challenge pupils, adding in something new or different, changing displays, mixing up themes and topics, creating cross-curricular connections. Removing the familiarity may slow the visible signs of progression but research suggests that it also stimulates the brain and in the long term improves retention.

Drawing on the work of several researchers and commentators – including Bjork – the following might support challenge that leads to deep learning:

- Inter-leaving topics so that pupils have to think about what they have previously learnt
- 'Low stakes' testing of interrelated learning rather than just recalling, re-reading or revising
- Asking learners to look at what they have learnt from a different perspective or through a different lens
- Changing where the learning takes place – in the school grounds, on a school visit, in the hall, sitting on the floor rather than at desks or tables
- Including learning props that are not familiar from previous lessons, for instance introducing photographs of topography while looking at how to read maps
- Using fonts that are unfamiliar or dual-coding where images represent text or the other way around

Challenge can also lead to failure or a lack of immediate success. Teachers need to develop within their pupils a mindset and a resilience that it is OK to make mistakes, to draw the wrong conclusion or to find the learning difficult. Where there is a culture that celebrates failure and mistakes as part of a process of learning more assured pupils are willing to take risks and are far more likely to find their own learning solutions (Sherrington, 2017).

To close this section on what we are assessing there is a final tool in the box that proves to be successful in ensuring pupils can achieve more and more – and probably a lot more than what is within the perception of the teacher: creating models of good practice, what does good writing look like, show the best constructions, the high jump technique, the use of colour in painting, a clay pot and so on and so on. Not the best from the class you have in front of you but from the past, from your own collection, from pictures online. A well-used and popular interpretation of this theory is Austin's butterfly (Berger, 2002). Repeated attempts at drawing a butterfly and an understanding of what a good drawing would look like improved Austin's final interpretation of the butterfly no end.

How are we assessing?

The how of assessment is pivotal in the determination of all curriculum content. It is at the planning stage that all those involved in the decisions about the subject content and how this is unveiled over time need to dovetail with the depth and breadth of the learning experience we want our pupils to have.

Deciding on the pedagogy that will ensure pupils learn well, remember, make connections and create new pathways for themselves needs to be a distinct factor in bringing together the different elements that will determine whether pupils have learnt the curriculum and mastered the standards. It is therefore essential that part of the assessment process should be a deep focus on the quality of teaching, the pedagogy that will determine how well pupils are progressing over time.

Formative assessment is the process by which the teacher and the pupil interact. The teacher is the conductor who carefully orchestrates their class and moves pupils to be stretched and challenged in relation to their capability and learning capacity. The teacher needs to know each and every member of the class. Data is a necessary part of this, but it is not a panacea. Data can be important, but it can also be misleading and create false assumptions about pupils which is limiting if it is relied on too much. Certainly, relying totally on grades will mean senior and subject leaders, teachers, parents and other stakeholders will have a raw and incomplete picture of each pupil's capacity for learning. Far better to create a classroom where the teacher is immersed in dialogue with pupils, where pupils work together as pairs or in groups in a mixed ability culture so that the teacher builds a rapport and all pupils see and have the opportunity to work with the most difficult and stimulating content.

One of the most important strategies for formative assessment is creating opportunities for dialogue with pupils. Where it is the pupils who talk about their learning, what they know what they can do and what they want to find out really helps to consolidate that learning and allows the teacher to hear first-hand how well they are grasping a concept or learning a new approach or are able to describe a sequence of events, explain how to solve a problem, analyse the reason for differences or a change in state, or evaluate a given situation.

Alison Peacock in her book *Assessment for Learning without Limits* devotes a chapter to listening: 'Learning to Listen: Finding a way through for every child'. She says:

> Connections in learning are crucially important to developing cognition. Often through dialogue, we gain insight into the child's emerging understanding in a way that cannot possibly be substituted through passive post-learning activity such as scrutinising

children's exercise books. It is important, therefore, to give children the opportunity to express their emerging understanding in a safe and non-judgemental environment. This environment should be founded on trust and include every member of the class. (Peacock, 2016:-18)

Giving pupils a voice in the pursuance of their learning works for all pupils not just those who have the privilege of highly interactive dialogue at home as well as at school. All pupils are curious, have different interests, maybe even passions such as football, Lego, dinosaurs, tractors, fossils. Creating opportunities for pupils to talk about themselves, their hobbies, their favourite pastimes, their games or, in fact, anything at all builds confidence and creates an understanding that to talk and to listen are the greatest tools we have at our disposal to support continuous learning and achievement.

Another sound practice is to allow pupils to assess each other's work. Peer-to-peer assessment must be encouraged in a positive and trusting environment where individual pupils share their ideas and are encouraged to offer constructive albeit simple feedback. Group work can also be a very positive way to assess learning; however, it is often not as successful as it could be. Pupils need to be taught how to work as a group and not just be placed in a group. Creating an awareness of what the group is aiming to achieve in terms of goal-setting, ensuring all members of the group know what they are expected to achieve as part of the team will all lead to effective group work. Where the teacher observes this in action there is a wealth of extremely useful information about learning.

Assessing the written word is much more than simply marking the spellings or checking that there is a beginning, a middle and an end. It is what is contained within the writing that counts and it is through conjunctions or synonyms that we can support pupils to think more deeply and write well to show evidence of their growing understanding and depth of knowledge. Where teachers understand the language of the taxonomy verbs within the standards provide the teacher with opportunities to prompt pupils to begin to use higher levels of response they will need later on in their curriculum journey. Discuss, identify, understand, explain differences are just a few that populate the curriculum standards. Asking questions to stretch the thinking and add weight to the written or spoken explanation will aid learning. What difference did it make? What happened next? What would make a difference here? How did that actually happen?

Quizzes and low-stakes testing have their place as an integral part of formative assessment. They reveal where pupils have remembered and hopefully learnt certain facts or information. They also reveal where there are misconceptions or a palpable lack of understanding at all. However, if these are simply used for the purpose of summative data they will not have the desired impact on learning that other forms of assessment might evoke. Pupils do seem to like these kinds of tests and want to know how well they have done. It is what they reveal in terms of how much knowledge has been retained, what is it that pupils haven't understood or have a complete misconception about. Ranking pupils following on from this kind of testing can have negative consequences so it is probably best not to.

Questioning is an art in the quest for highly motivating and challenging feedback. The way teachers pose a question can have a dramatic impact on building the self-esteem of pupils as well as creating the right conditions that allow for thinking deeply, developing arguments, assessing what next or what for.

Learning how to use questioning successfully is a powerful skill that should be an essential element of any strategic plan for teachers' CPD. Where teachers learn to what extent questioning can make a difference to learning, to progression and to challenging learners towards higher levels of response there is a measurable difference in how well pupils perform.

The essential nature of how the teacher poses the question is crucial. Firstly, it is paramount that all those with a pupil-facing role understand the difference between asking a closed question or an open question can make. Secondly, the question has the power to encourage or dampen down enthusiasm and so learning how to ask questions that motivate and lead to the desire to find out more or choose a new approach is important. Thirdly, questioning provides the teacher with the tools to assess understanding, probe for misconceptions and build confidence in taking a risk that the answer might be wrong but might be leading the pupil in the right direction.

Open questions are those that cannot evoke a yes or no response. It sounds easy but it is my experience that the default is frequently to the closed question. An open question can only begin with one of these six words:

- Why
- What
- When
- How
- Which
- Where

What are your reasons for choosing that material? It is not possible to answer yes or no and requires an answer that clarifies understanding of the suitability of a particular material in a given situation.

When will you know that it is ready? Again the answer cannot evoke a yes or no answer but requires a focus on how long and an assessment of what is the right length of time.

Which way do you think will be the quickest? For this question the questioner might be looking for an answer that is not necessarily straightforward. A map may show one way that might look the quickest, but in fact isn't because of a range of hills, going through a town, a single road as opposed to a motorway and so on.

How do you know that is the right answer, the right way, the most useful and so on, probes for much greater clarity that the pupil has understood and is on the right track.

Be careful with the word why. Why did you think that was a good idea? Why did you choose that method? Why didn't you do it that way? These are all open questions but could be demotivating and judgemental.

Closed questions have their place and can help to clarify, refine and confirm. Such questions are: 'Did you try all the different approaches?' 'Can you explain why that one has worked so well?' 'Could you think of any other ways to do that?' 'Would you be able to use any other materials for the same task?' All of these questions can invite a yes or no answer but hopefully will lead to deeper thinking and a full and rounded response.

Feedback is the engine that drives progression. There must be a constant and very positive focus on what pupils are learning, how they are constantly building on existing learning and adding new bits of learning. Without this the process of acquiring new knowledge has no real meaning for the pupil and for the teacher no fulfilment that their planning and pedagogy are making a difference.

However, let us look a little more closely at the concept of 'feedforward' rather than feedback. If, as teachers, we focus on what pupils have already produced, discussed or written about as an end in itself it is difficult for them to concentrate on what they can do about it. Their efforts and their performance are being judged, fairly or unfairly. If, instead, we use what has already been produced to emphasise what they have achieved so far as a work in progress and provide a feedforward approach that asks incisive questions to foster further enquiry, discussion, shared fact-finding or a genuine desire to make changes then we have not dampened down any enthusiasm for continuing to learn and deepen understanding.

In his book *The Feedback Fix: Dump the Past, Embrace the Future, Lead the Way to Change* Jo Hirsch (2017) talks about feedforward as the way to encourage progression and create opportunities for genuine reflection that lead to self-awareness and self-improvement. He uses the word 'repair' to marshal thoughts on feedforward.

- *Regenerates* talent
- *Expands* possibilities
- Is *particular* and not generic
- Is *authentic*
- Has *impact*
- *Refines* thinking

So feedforward is a focus on the positive – it aims to build self-esteem and creates a learning culture. This approach fosters a genuine passion for learning that is infectious across the whole class, the whole year group, phase or subject specialism. It seeps into whole-school philosophies and builds confidence, creativity and a consistent desire for continuous improvement. The pedagogy to put this positive approach into practice still requires teachers to be highly skilled in the art of positive questioning. It is in the way the teacher assesses the learning that is taking place that makes the difference.

- Excellent ideas. 'How can you say more?'
- Good work so far. 'What else is there to add in here?'
- I like the shape of this. 'Who else could we involve?'
- I enjoyed what I read. 'What else could you do now to build on this idea?'
- Some good findings here. 'Where might you go next?'

Creating a culture within a school where teachers and pupils know that they have the potential towards continuous improvement, a forever learning attitude is most definitely enhanced through always looking forward to the next steps in learning.

How do we know assessment has an impact on learning?

This chapter focuses on assessment as an integral part of the planning and implementation process of excellent curriculum design and outstanding pedagogical application. The teacher must have a profound understanding as to the content that is to be delivered in the pursuance of high-quality teaching and learning. He or she must see the bigger picture and define what will be assessed in relation to subject and conceptual knowledge, the sequencing of the learning and skills pupils will develop as an integral part of their journey.

So, in order for assessment to have an impact, it must be closely aligned with the planned outcomes that are defined in the learning goals for lessons or a series of lessons and in the wider curriculum planning process. Simply marking books or using summative testing at the end of a topic, term, year or key stage tells us something about what has been remembered but has little regard to the nuances of learning. It also provides us with a rather depressing understanding of what pupils have misunderstood, completely forgotten or where there are distinct gaps in learning. Where assessment is a part of the everyday lesson the teacher can continually review the learning that is taking place. Effective questioning can elicit how well the pupil has understood and where the gaps are in their learning as part of every lesson. There are opportunities to find ways to ensure pupils have fully understood and ensure that glaring misconceptions are avoided. By the end of a topic, it is too late to put right where pupils have not fully understood.

It is therefore essential to build an assessment policy that is formative, where reflection is a key element of the process. In this way the teacher can use specific times to find out more about pupils' understanding, reinforce some key points and through good questioning with individuals, in groups and as a whole class can assess how well pupils are absorbing their learning and making sure that they want to learn more.

Assessment is having an impact if it encourages progression and builds confidence so that pupils are happy to make mistakes, take risks and find their own solutions.

Where there is a culture of positivity that rewards effort, looks beyond the production of a piece of written work or final product to the methods used, the discussions that fostered ideas and the shared learning that led there then learning is celebrated and pupils will make progress with an air of confidence and self-belief.

Conclusion

Assessment must be seen as an integral part of the curriculum planning process. Where it is clear what outcomes teachers want from their teaching and what they want their pupils to learn and remember as they unfold the curriculum content over time there are profound opportunities to make meaningful judgements as to the impact curriculum implementation is having on their pupils. Assessment of the learning is also a critical test of the quality of the pedagogy and the opportunities for pupil interaction in the classroom. No teacher should underestimate the power of continuing and positive formative assessment has on the outcomes pupils are capable of producing.

Summative assessment, especially where it is 'low stakes', has a place and many pupils benefit from informal testing and quizzing. It is clear, however, that assessment should not be purely a tool for assessing how well pupils will achieve in external tests at the end of Key Stage 1 and 2. More importantly, it is essential that there are opportunities for reflective practice where teachers ask the questions, 'How has my teaching impacted on learning? How do I know that I am making a difference?

Cognitive science reveals the importance of recall, practice and making connections across all learning and all teachers, whether new or experienced, will benefit from collective discussions that ask the question, 'What is learning? Teachers need to think about the learning process and how pupils are deepening their learning over time.

Finally, it is so important to build in time to ask the questions of all teaching staff and their support teams: What are we assessing? How are we assessing? and How is assessment impacting on learning?

Top tips

- Create opportunities for teams to work together to plan backwards so that the end goal is the starting point and where assessment of the learning is integral
- Be clear as to the difference between formative and summative assessment and the purpose and impact of both
- Build in time for moderation and a shared commitment to ensuring all pupil-facing staff can identify exemplar material that champions excellence across a range of subjects and topics
- Emphasise the theory of cognitive science in the deepening of understanding of the science and art of learning, memory and progression towards mastery

- Insist that literacy and numeracy are seen as tools that support the access to knowledge in every subject and their relevance is not just emphasised in English and maths
- Expect to see an element of challenge as an integral part of every lesson or series of lessons
- Create subject and cross-curricular teams that transcend year groups and key stages to foster a synergy in assessment planning
- Encourage professional learning conversations about thinking skills, metacognition and cross-curricular applications that support learning
- Create a culture where mistakes are an integral part of the learning process
- Foster a culture that encourages opportunities for pupils to do the talking about their learning

References

Abbot, J. (1994) *Learning Makes Sense: Re-creating Education for a Changing Future*. Letchworth: Education 200.

Berger, R. (2012) *Lessons from Austin's Butterfly*. New York: EL Education. Available at: https://eleducation.org/resources/austins-butterfly (accessed 27 July 2022).

Bjork, R. A. (1994) 'Institutional impediments to effective training'. In Druckman, D. and Bjork, R. A. (eds) *Learning, Remembering, Believing: Enhancing Human Performance*. Washington, DC: National Academy Press, pp. 295–306.

Black, P. and Wiliam, D. (1998) *Inside the Black Box: Raising Standards through Classroom Assessment*. London: GL Assessment/King's College London School of Education.

Christodoulou, D. (2016) *Making Good Progress? The Future of Assessment for Learning*. Oxford: Oxford University Press.

Department for Education (DfE) (2014) *National Curriculum in England: Framework for Key Stages 1 and 2*. London: DfE.

Didau, D. (2016) *What If Everything You Knew about Education was Wrong?* Carmarthen: Crown House Publishing.

Education Endowment Foundation (2018) *Metacognition and Self-Regulated Learning*. London: Education Endowment Foundation.

Harford, S. (2018) *Assessment – what are inspectors looking for?* Blog OFSTED

Hirsch, J. (2017) *The Feedback Fix: Dump the Past, Embrace the Future, Lead the Way to Change*. Lanham, MD: Rowman & Littlefield.

Institute of Education (2002) 'Effective Learning', *NSIN Research Matters*, 17 (Summer 2002).

Kolb, D. A. (1984) *Experiential Learning: Experience as the Source of Learning and Development.* Englewood Cliffs, N.J. Prentice-Hill.

Ofsted (2022) *School Inspection Handbook*. London: Ofsted.

Peacock, A. (2016) *Assessment for Learning without Limits*. London: Open University Press, McGraw-Hill Education.

Sherrington, T. (2017) *The Learning Rainforest – Great Teaching in Real Classrooms*. Woodbridge: John Catt Educational.

Wiliam, D. (2011) *Embedded Formative Assessment*. Bloomington: Solution Tree Press.

8

CURRICULUM COHESION – A SCHOOL IN SYNERGY

If there is agreement that the curriculum model is the progression model, and we ensure that our policies meet the two tests of impact and workload, then it is possible to refocus energies into designing an effective curriculum. Senior leaders therefore have a responsibility to articulate that curriculum is where teacher energy is most effectively invested by ensuring the support mechanisms are there to enable them to do so. (Howard and Hill, 2020)

Leadership and pulling the threads together

Creating the right culture that fosters excellence in teaching and learning must be the absolute goal of the school leader and the teams they guide towards realisation of that goal. The essence of this is bound up in a belief that every child deserves the best from their very first experience of school in or before the early years and all the way through their primary years in preparation for transition to their secondary school. In this chapter we will focus on some of the research and best practice that create the school where quality and what it means in relation to the highest possible standards are part of a collective and ongoing conversation.

This must exist where the curriculum is at the heart of a learning culture where continuous professional development deepens subject knowledge and allows all staff to work together towards a common goal or vision. Also, where teachers are reflective, innovative and creative in their planning and pedagogy and who believe every child has the capacity to thrive in their endeavours and can achieve their potential over time.

Senior leaders define the vision through their deep understanding of the local and wider context within which their school is placed. They work closely with other stakeholders to draw together the main elements that will translate into a curriculum that will deliver balance and breadth. The leaders, however, must let go of the baton and leave their subject and phase leaders and their teams of teachers and support staff to take on the role of designing the curriculum offer within and across subjects. It is their expertise and close liaison with pupils that will ultimately deliver depth, breadth and curriculum cohesion.

Throughout this book I have emphasised the importance of a collective approach to defining the curriculum vision, planning how to implement a cohesive, sequential and conceptual delivery model in subjects and across the wider curriculum, and finding the right way to assess the impact on learning and achievement. Creating the right culture where professional conversations shape a collective determination of what works well and what can be improved upon is the only way forward to ensure evidence that all staff work in synergy. Here we will focus on a couple of the powerful ways that this collaboration can be achieved and in particular the creation within a school of professional learning communities that work together to realise the school vision and intent.

Research and the importance of collaboration

The curriculum and how well it is implemented has become a very important measure of success for a school. It is the fulcrum by which the quality of education is judged. The curriculum is, according to Amanda Spielman, the 'substance' of education (Spielman, 2017) in her commentary on the initial findings of research into primary and secondary curriculum design the final version of which was published in 2018. (Ofsted, 2018). It is true that the curriculum is important and is, essentially, the raw material teachers use to help pupils to learn and to create for them self-belief and a desire to process knowledge and develop a range of skills that will sustain them into secondary school and beyond.

> Effective communication to all stakeholders throughout a change process will promote, if not guarantee, success; ineffective communication is the biggest single cause of failure in all researched change projects. Any change project depends on the success of enabling individuals to change their behaviours, skills, attitudes or knowledge and that change will only take place if individuals are given time and space to articulate their feelings, concerns and hopes for change to others.
>
> Case (2005: 51)

In Chapter 3 there is a detailed look at the research undertaken by Ofsted in June 2019 especially focusing on lesson observation, the quality of education and the need for structured professional conversations to ensure there is a clear understanding that all those involved can interpret the intent and turn it into a seamless curriculum offer from Early Years to Year 6.

Ultimately, the curriculum is a group of subjects and the depth to which teachers must try to delve is laid out in the core and foundation programmes of study. We know from previous chapters that it is not a good idea to take these in isolation and allow individual teachers across different year groups or subjects to plan for their own class or develop subject specific study for one year.

So, it is to the third edge of this triangular piece of research that we look at in most depth for the purpose of this chapter in terms of how the primary school can pull all the threads together. The synergy that is required in order that the curriculum is delivered as a seamless process from Early Years to Year 6 must be driven by highly qualified and well-trained professionals who can work together as a team and build a consensus on what will be taught, how it will be taught and how it will be assessed. Ofsted have recognised in this piece of research the importance and value of the professional conversation, without which it is difficult to pull the threads together.

> Conversations with leaders, teachers and pupils can provide the vital context we need to understand what we see. These conversations are central to the deep dive model. However, relying purely on what people tell us would be problematic in an inspection

context. This is why we need first-hand evidence from pupils' work and lesson visits among other sources, such as attainment in national tests.

(Ofsted (2019) Assessing education quality)

The 'deep dive' questions that frame the inspection process are carefully crafted and aimed at finding out to what extent the curriculum intent is translated into a model of implementation that will deliver curriculum depth and breadth, allow pupils to progress and achieve and ascertain that there is a consistent message across subjects, year groups and key stages. The only way to ensure that this is happening is to create opportunities for subject leaders and their teams to work together and talk together.

The Teaching Schools Council's report from 2016 reinforces the importance of a collaborative approach to professional development. They say Effective Professional Development is:

- Focused on improving and evaluating pupil outcomes: with explicit relevance to partici-pants, linking activities to the intended outcomes and including ongoing evaluation of how changes impact those outcomes
- Underpinned by robust evidence and expertise: developing practice and theory together to enhance teachers' subject knowledge and challenge their understanding of teaching and how children learn
- Collaborative and challenged by experts: supported by external feedback, peer support and networks to improve programmes
- Sustained over time: with opportunities for experimentation, reflection, feedback and evaluation
- Prioritised by school leadership: with leaders modelling and championing effective professional development as an expectation for all, and ensuring that the necessary time and resource is available to implement it

Teaching Schools Council (2016) *Effective Primary Teaching Practice*

The pivotal role of the subject leader

The subject leader must work closely with the senior leadership team in order that he or she is aware of the school vision, the curriculum intent and the ambition the school leadership team has for all pupils as they progress towards Year 6 and beyond. Their role is also to lead their team and to translate the vision and intent into clearly defined subject and phase objectives that match the intent and deliver high-quality outcomes.

The subject leader or expert wears a number of hats including assessor, team leader, researcher, facilitator, influencer, translator, curriculum design expert, CPD coordina-tor, teacher, observer and more. Their ability to coordinate and to create the synergy required to ensure that their team or teams can answer the 'deep dive' questions that senior leaders, governors or inspectors might ask is essential.

In order to develop their teams, the subject leader or expert must be able to translate the curriculum into subject-specific learning. They must be able to manage change where individual team members are reluctant to think differently or try out new approaches. The role involves the need to influence a consistent approach across the learning spectrum so that high-quality outcomes are guaranteed in every classroom, year group and key stage.

> The world we have created is a product of our own thinking: it cannot be changed without changing our thinking. (Einstein)

Change is likely to be a constant and understanding how individuals react is a powerful leadership skill. Cynthia Scott and Dennis Jaffe (1988) developed a useful change model for the education sector that replicates the bereavement curve and focuses on how individuals react to change over time (see Figure 8.1). Moving from denial and resistance to exploration and commitment requires good management and a profound understanding of how people react and feel when change threatens the status quo.

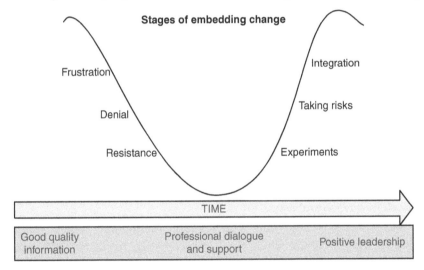

Figure 8.1 An interpretation of Scott and Jaffe's change model diagram

In order to create curriculum cohesion, it is up to the subject leader to coordinate and pull all the strands together to create the balance between realising the curriculum vision and creating the strategy that will allow his or her team to plan and implement high-quality curriculum outcomes in a way that ensures everyone involved embraces change positively. A good starting point is to use the questions below:

- What are the essential points that need to be conveyed in relation to making sure the team has a profound understanding of the school vision and intent?
- What strategies are in place to ensure that teachers from across phases and year groups can work together to plan a sequence of learning from Early Years to Year 6?

- Can all staff articulate and define the vocabulary of the curriculum?
- How are literacy and numeracy embedded within the subject being taught?
- For English and maths subject leads, how do they make sure that literacy and numeracy are integral to learning in all subjects?
- What are the mechanisms for making sure that all teachers have the expertise to teach depth and breadth in a range of subjects?
- How do phase and subject leaders work together to define what is meant by quality in relation to the implementation of the curriculum?
- What is planned to ensure that pupils with Special Needs and Disabilities can access the widest curriculum and are not disadvantaged in pursuit of depth and breadth of learning?
- What is required to create a consistent and accurate system of assessing learning and progress?

Developing highly effective teams that will support subject leaders to make the right decisions and who can work together to achieve the vision does require that they understand the strengths within their teams. Conversely, they must also know where there may be gaps in their knowledge, their experience and their ability to deliver. Where members of the team are encouraged to articulate and celebrate their strengths and are able without judgement to know their professional development needs in order to fill the gaps in their knowledge and expertise the team will inevitably work together in an atmosphere of trust and a shared desire to learn and be successful in their endeavours.

Team working and the curriculum deep dive

The term 'deep dive' has become synonymous with ensuring the curriculum has a synergy that can be articulated by all those who are part of the process of planning how and what to teach and assess.

Essentially, the phrase asks that school senior, middle and subject leaders in a school are creating a culture where they empower their teams to work together to achieve a consensus on the rationale for the choices being made as to the ambition and realisation of the curriculum they plan and deliver. The deep dive is a good analogy, although it conjures up some of the worst images of inspectors turning up in flippers and goggles. It suggests immersion in a belief that the right curriculum will deliver high-quality learning and create strategies that lead to higher pupil attainment and achievement.

A deep dive comes in the form of a suite of questions that a team leader, line manager or inspector might ask in an appraisal, as part of a lesson observation or in a series of coaching sessions. It is a lens on how the highest-level strategic thinking translates into what is happening in the classroom, which aligns with the vision and intent and reveals that all those planning and delivering the curriculum know the part they play in the process of implementation.

The team must work together with a shared commitment to deliver the highest-quality outcomes. Each member of the team must have the skills and motivation to work with their colleagues and articulate the steps that will need to be taken to achieve the stated goals, evaluate and celebrate successes along the way, and grow in their own professional learning as part of the process.

For the purposes of internal planning consider the simple model in Figure 8.2, Learning Cultures Limited (Stansfield, 2022) Coaching for Middle Leaders.

Figure 8.2 The Five Ps of Creating a Team Approach to Creating Curriculum Synergy
(Learning Cultures, 2022)

Here, teams can work together to focus on their own strengths, qualities and personalities that will lead to the celebration of their stated goals and objectives. This approach can also provide opportunities for team or subject leaders to use a suite of deep dive questions to support the journey from stating the goal to evaluating the impact of the journey towards success for pupils, teachers and the school.

The purpose is, of course, the goal, the intent, the rationale, the vision or the ambition the school has for each and every learner in their charge. This requires deep discussion prior to internal reflection or external scrutiny and must be SMART (specific, measurable, achievable, realistic and time related) in how it is translated to all those who play a part in delivering it. The senior leadership team should have clear answers to similar questions as these:

- What are the factors that have influenced the design of your curriculum?
- How ambitious is your curriculum in ensuring that it embraces the potential of all pupils?
- What are the essential elements that will ensure all pupils achieve and exceed their potential?
- How does the curriculum reflect the wider school vision and rationale?
- What strategies are in place to ensure that the curriculum is sequential and allows for progression from Early Years to Year 6 and beyond?
- How will you measure how well pupils build on prior learning, develop positive skills especially in reading and numeracy, and can make connections across all their learning?
- What are the mechanisms for ensuring all subject leaders, teachers and teaching assistants have the essential skills and resources to deliver the curriculum intent?
- How will you measure the impact of the curriculum on learning, progression and achievement?

All staff must have the skills, the motivation and the expert knowledge of the curriculum to play their part in building high-quality learning experiences. It is to subject leaders and their teams to work together to ensure they have the answers to similar questions to these:

- How does the team work together to ensure all elements within their subject specific programme of study are covered?
- What is in place to ensure that there is a collaborative approach to ensuring that subject teams work with their colleagues to see where there is synergy in other subjects?
- How is the curriculum planned to ensure there is a clear framework for progression?
- What is in place to ensure all pupils build on prior learning and retain subject specific and conceptual knowledge and skills?
- How are teachers and others working together to ensure there is a deep understanding of how their pedagogy ensures pupils acquire the knowledge and skills within each subject and in the wider curriculum?
- How does assessment both formative and summative provide evidence that pupils have a deep understanding of the curriculum and are building their knowledge over time?
- How is continuing professional development linked to ensuring all staff have the skills and expertise to deliver a high-quality curriculum?

The process or how the curriculum is implemented has the potential to be something that the teacher has the responsibility for and there is a danger that the communication necessary to ensure the sequencing of learning and the required depth of knowledge and skills development is an individual's responsibility. This would impede the ability of a school to demonstrate that there is a synergy and a collective responsibility for a sequential and progressive curriculum offer. In order to answer the following questions a team approach and opportunities for regular reflection and deep professional discussion is essential.

- How do we ensure depth and breadth of subject coverage, intentional progression and the sequencing of knowledge and skills over time?
- What is the evidence that what is being taught marries with the school vision and intent for high-quality learning in all subjects and across the curriculum?
- How do we ensure the sequence of learning is not broken at times of transition?
- What measures are in place to ensure that there is a consistency of provision across all subjects?
- How do we measure that pupils are deepening and retaining their knowledge over time?
- How is assessment planned as part of a learning sequence and how are pupils who are falling behind or need to be challenged identified for support?
- How is data used to share pupils' progress and address any issues that arise?
- How do teachers across the different core and foundation subjects ensure pupils have a deep subject and conceptual vocabulary that grows over time?
- How do we measure whether teachers have sufficient depth and breadth of curriculum and subject knowledge?
- What is in place to ensure continuing professional learning and development are integral to the process of curriculum implementation?

The product is all about the culture the school is creating that enables all pupils to learn, to progress and to be ready for the next stage of their education. The questions probe for evidence of profound learning, engaged and motivated pupils and well-trained and creative staff. These might include:

- How do classrooms, corridors and other spaces reflect the learning and the value of the curriculum across all year groups?
- How is progression measured in books and in other media such as design products, artwork, prowess on the sports field, in music performances or drama and dance sequences?
- What opportunities are there for teachers to share their own good and outstanding prac-tice with others?
- How does continuing professional development impact on learning and achievement?
- How does the school embrace the wider community in building a learning culture?

The prize or the impact of how the curriculum is implemented must be celebrated and all those involved should know that their contribution has made a significant difference to the life chances of every pupil in the school. These questions may help to ensure that at all times it is essential to recognise the value of all those involved in the school's success.

- How does the school share the accomplishments of pupils at certain points along the year, at the end of the year and at the end of each key stage?
- What is in place so that pupils know and can celebrate their own achievements, however small or large?
- What happens to the work that pupils have produced at the end of a year or key stage, how is their best piece of work shared with others?
- What kind of graduation process exists so that pupils feel their own right of passage from one year or key stage to the next?

The power of the professional learning community (PLC)

Creating a curriculum requires strategic approaches to ongoing collaboration and the role of formalised professional learning communities (PLC) can be highly beneficial. A PLC is a group of people who work together with one sole purpose in mind. The make-up of the group is carefully chosen to represent the expertise and skills required to achieve a particular goal linked to a specific and clearly defined strategy. The first and most important role for the group is to establish a common goal and to make sure those chosen to be a part of the PLC have the skills and expertise to make a meaning-ful contribution to its achievement.

Once established the group can work together to focus on what is currently working well and how good practice can form the basis of what will be built upon in order to deliver high-quality curriculum outcomes. The PLC group must also understand the barriers they might encounter as they work towards their stated goal or goals. Sharing potential pitfalls such as deficits in subject expertise, a lack of clarity in relation to curriculum vocabulary, a lack of understanding of how to teach the age-related standards and a lack of understanding as to the importance of ongoing formative assessment all might impede progress and require decisions outside the group's remit to allow some staff to access the CPD they need to make up any shortfall in their knowledge and expertise.

In the case of developing a cohesive approach to ensuring the curriculum is well-planned and delivers high-quality learning it is clear that there will be a number of teams who will work on specific subjects and themes. English, maths and science have very specific standards with which to work. The PLC for each of these needs to consist of individuals from each year group and phase within the school. For larger multi-form entry schools there may be a need for there to be both a Key Stage 1 and Key Stage 2 team working separately on the core curriculum within their specific key stage. In this case there is an absolute imperative to make sure that the teams can knit together what happens across the transition bridge from Key Stage 1 to 2.

> Teams have great potential for solving hard problems in challenging contexts. They bring together more skills, knowledge and experience to work than any single individual can. They can integrate individual members' diverse contributions into a creative problem and that is what is needed ... The challenge is to identify what it takes for teams to maximise their potential. (Aguilar, 2016: 7)

Where the group can work together to understand the standards that have to be taught, when they will be introduced and in what depth, they become increasingly familiar with the content of the curriculum in terms of the breadth of study and can also focus on the imperative to include what will be assessed and when.

Working collaboratively, teachers can share their interpretation and begin to reach an agreement on the key elements of the overarching curriculum vocabulary. It is this collective knowledge that will ensure even the very new teacher is exposed to the deepest knowledge of the curriculum within the school. The collaborative voice that emerges is likely to have profound and well-structured answers to any questions that might be asked about how the curriculum is being delivered.

Sharing the outcome of the PLC's work in terms of developing a sequential curriculum for science, maths and English can then be cascaded to those who are charged with developing medium- and long-term plans for all of the foundation subjects. There are clear links and obvious overlaps between subjects such as English, history and RE or maths, science and geography, and where individuals from the core teams work closely with the foundation teams the opportunity to continue to look in detail at how to embed literacy, numeracy and skills such as enquiry, group work and analysis can be looked at using a collective expertise. In the same way a PLC dedicated to design technology could work in unison with art or music with drama.

The make-up of the PLC may vary as the curriculum plans develop and change over time. The focus must be on creating a synergy where every team understands the part they play in the continuous process of curriculum implementation, assessment and review. It is potentially time-consuming but there is no substitute for providing these opportunities for a shared focus on creating progressive learning platforms within and across subjects and building a consensus as to the depth and breadth necessary to ensure learning is guaranteed. The secret is in insisting that this kind of team approach is actually part of a CPD strategy and therefore can be an essential element of meeting time, twilight training time and INSET days designed for training and development. The key here is to emphasise that all schools exist for learning, for pupils most definitely, but also for every member of staff and sometimes even embracing the local community, the governors and most certainly parents and carers.

The DfE's Standards for Teachers' Professional Development which were published in 2016 have five strands:

- Professional development should have a focus on improving and evaluating pupil outcomes
- Professional development should be underpinned by robust evidence and expertise
- Professional development should include collaboration and expert challenge
- Professional development programmes should be sustained over time
- Professional development must be prioritised by the school leadership

The third of these also emphasises the importance of collaboration and expert challenge.

Other evidence that supports this approach can be found in the research undertaken by the Education Endowment Foundation (EEF) into effective CPD strategies where the focus on collaborative learning approaches such as Professional (Teacher) Learning Communities, the use of lesson study and instructional coaching are all cited as examples of positive strategies for ongoing professional learning. The EEF Teaching and Learning Toolkit also includes collaborative learning approaches as being low-cost and high-impact strategies for improving teaching and learning.

The role of coaching in the success of the PLC

Coaching is transformational, it is an approach that ensures that individuals contain the process within which they are working and remain close to the detail. Developing a range of coaching skills will ensure that all those working together have the opportunity to reflect on their contribution, focus on resolving issues that are causing blocks and build on the positive steps towards the progress that the group is making. Creating a team of coaches who can support members of a PLC to articulate their goals for success, share their progress towards realising their objectives and discuss obstacles and barriers and how these might be overcome is inspirational and works.

There are several possibilities that might provide the best way forward in who should train to coach others. It may be that there are already trained coaches in school. One possibility is to build a team of coaches who are also subject or phase leaders. They can then coach their own team. One idea that I have seen work in the past is for a trained coach/subject leader to train members of a team other than their own. In this way there is the possibility of greater objectivity. The role of the coach is to be a critical friend and a good listener and be able to ask the kinds of questions that will lead the coachee (person being coached) to find their own solution. Where the subject leader is coaching his or her own team members there may be conflicts of interest that make the process lack impartiality. It may be that the coaching team are separate from the curriculum teams and are therefore simply there to provide a listening ear and to build self-esteem where the focus is on achieving the priorities that are linked to the original goals set by the team and by the individuals within it.

There are many primary schools which are very small, one-form entry schools where subject teams overlap or are made up of just one or two individuals. Formal coaching may not be possible in this situation. Informal opportunities for professional conversations where individuals can share their progress and define where they are along the journey to achieving success can be just as valuable.

Whatever the situation, it is the opportunity to share ideas, discuss what is working well and articulate the barriers that impede progress. Where individuals talk in this structured way, whether through formal coaching sessions or informal professional conversations, they are deepening their awareness of their own strengths and successes and can see more clearly the next steps in the process. Articulating a shared goal sharpens the desire to achieve, deepens the resolve to find solutions and helps to overcome barriers that may seem insurmountable when not shared.

Coaching skills that will support curriculum cohesion

Creating curriculum cohesion is not easy across several year groups, key stages and a range of very different core and foundation subjects. In order to create a truly cohesive and collaborative school where everyone with a pupil-facing role knows the part they play in realising the vision and intent requires considerable effort and carefully structured leadership strategies. Creating a coaching team will be a decision that will reap benefits in relation to providing the mechanism by which all staff have a point of reference and a critical friend.

However, coaching is a skill and needs nurturing and honing over time. In order to become a coach there are three main elements that need to be in place: coaches must have a range of relevant coaching skills, they must decide on the process they want to use with individuals and teams to coach them successfully, and they must have a range of qualities that Christian van Nieuwerburgh in his book, *An Introduction to Coaching Skills: A Practical Guide*, describes as 'ways of being' (van Nieuwerburgh, 2014: 10).

The first and possibly most important skill a coach must learn is to listen actively and accurately. When someone listens attentively it is a sign of respect and trust and gives the person being listened to the confidence to say more and to open up to sharing their innermost fears or anxieties and to celebrating their successes and articulating their strengths.

The second most important skill a coach needs is to be able to ask really deep and incisive questions. They need to know when to use open questions that challenge and where a yes or no answer is not an option, and when to use closed questions to dampen down a conversation or to move forward with the conversation to another issue or matter.

Examples of open questions – where the answer cannot be yes or no:

How would you explain your decision? What encouraged you to work towards that outcome? When will you complete this stage of the project? Where else could you go to find out more? Which method do you think will work best?

Examples of closed questions – can evoke a yes or no answer and are definitive:

Do you think that will work? Can you find another way to do that? Should you be happy with that outcome? Could you find a different approach?

The deep dive questions used earlier in this chapter are all examples of open questions and may be very useful for senior and middle leaders who want to use coaching skills in their pursuit of creating the synergy they hope for. We look at open and closed questions in the classroom in Chapter 7 which may also be useful.

Questioning is an art form and there are many ways to ask questions. Becoming adept at knowing how to ask the right question in the right situation makes for a challenging classroom where pupils are exposed to challenge and made to think very carefully about their responses. So, apart from the open questions discussed above and closed questions such as 'Have you finished?' 'Are you enjoying this approach?' explore these other questioning types taken from an activity designed by Learning Cultures in their Middle Leader Coaching Programme:

Table 8.1 Different approaches to asking the right questions

Probing questions	Where is there more information about this? What else could you do with this?
Leading questions	What can you add in here to finish this piece of work? What do you think you could do to make sure you arrived on time?
Funnel questions	What was it that made you interested in this? What did you like most about this approach?
Recall questions	What can you remember from the last lesson? What else have you learnt about that is similar?
Rhetorical questions	What colour is Monday? How deep is the ocean?

A useful and simple model that can be revised and used in all sorts of situations from formal CPD to appraisal or with pupils in the classroom is:

What	......are the learning outcomes you want to achieve?
	......do you already know that you can build on here?
	......do you need to do now to add to your current understanding?
	......do you need to do to find out more?
So what	......have you learnt so far?
	......are the next steps?
	......else can you contribute?
	......is your new understanding?
Now what	.......will you do to build on your current understanding?
	......will learning the skills be useful for in the future?
	......might you do differently now you know about this?
	......might be the consequences of not using my new knowledge and skills?

Learning how to ask the right questions for different situations has many advantages. For the school leader deep and incisive questioning creates a culture where individuals know that they have to find their own solutions, solve their own problems and create their own pathways to success. Where teams work together towards a common goal, questioning can provide the clarity of purpose and ensure there is team cohesion. In the classroom, effective questioning challenges pupils to think for themselves, allows pupils to know what they need to do to improve their work and ensures that there is less reliance on the teacher to have all the answers.

Using a coaching model can help to create a framework for which to define the goal and the way forward towards successful outcomes. One of the most well-used and useful models is the GROW model, first introduced by John Whitmore in his book *Coaching for Performance* (Whitmore, 2017).

- **Goal** – what is the goal that clearly defines the way forward?
- **Reality** – what is working well and what might be the barriers that get in the way of success?
- **Options** – what are the different options that will guarantee success?
- **Will** – what will be the first thing you do and when?

Where the coach uses GROW to support team members to plan and achieve their goals and strategies there is an opportunity to ask deep and challenging questions that will help to move the process forward.

Instructional coaching as a tool for continuous improvement

The term 'instructional coaching' is increasingly being used in relation to CPD and school improvement strategies in England. It is an American derivative of coaching, very much adopted by the educationalist Jim Knight (2007). Specifically, the word instructional is used because in the USA the word instruction is synonymous with the word pedagogy. For those who, like myself, find the word instructional to be the complete opposite of coaching it is useful to use the alternative phrase incremental coaching. Incremental suggests a step-by-step approach to improving practice and deepening understanding or a set of steps that lead to the achievement of a goal or set of objectives. The term and the philosophy behind the idea of incremental or – for the purist – instructional coaching provide an opportunity to develop a CPD strategy that will create the cohesion and collective vision for curriculum success.

The role of the 'incremental' coach is to support the process of learning for the teacher or team who are developing the curriculum plan and putting it into practice in the classroom. Finding ways to weave together the many layers of understanding and to build sequential and conceptual knowledge over time does require a level of understanding of the curriculum standards and how these are interpreted by individuals that make up the several curriculum teams likely to be working towards a shared or common goal.

The coach must have the skills to help individuals and teams to realise their professional goals in relation to curriculum delivery. The coach in this context must have a broad repertoire of best practice built through research, a shared understanding of what is working well in the school and perhaps where groups of schools are part of a partnership gathering evidence from other schools. However, there is more at stake for the coach than simply knowing what best practice looks like and sharing it. In terms of the PLC set up to tackle the complex issues surrounding how to create a curriculum that will deliver all of the elements that have been discussed in several previous chapters in this book, the coach must work with the individuals and the team to determine the priorities that must be met in the realisation of the defined goals. The focus for the coach needs to be clear otherwise there is a danger that time will be wasted on trying to sort out too many issues at once. There are possibly four or five potential issues that can be separated out in order that they can then be dovetailed together as the plan finally comes to fruition. These are:

- The individual contribution and performance of each member of the team
- A deep understanding by all team members of the component parts of the curriculum mapping process, the standards, the knowledge, the sequence of learning, the conceptual processes within and across subjects and the skills that pupils need to develop and use
- The pedagogy that supports learning and progression and how this is planned in relation to the curriculum content
- A cohesive and consistent approach to assessment and how through a collective and shared understanding of taxonomies and rubrics teachers can assess pupils' progress accurately in a range of different subjects and along the trajectory of years and key stages
- A fifth issue is data collection and how it is used to judge the progress of pupils, the quality of output in certain subjects and the quality of teaching or pedagogy

Creating for individuals within the team a sense of purpose around each of the above builds a sense of belonging, a belief that they can achieve their goals and a resilience to continue to work towards the desired outcome even when the going gets tough. In this context, the coach's role is to create opportunities to build incremental steps towards success and encourage reflection and positive attitudes to change and challenge along the way. Creating this kind of culture will support the development of outstanding curriculum outcomes that are built on a spirit of partnership and collaboration.

Conclusion

Creating the right conditions where PLCs can flourish will provide the essential evidence that there is a collaborative approach to curriculum design and delivery. The concept of a 'deep dive' to ascertain how well the curriculum is being delivered and whether the impact it has on pupils and learning correspond with the schools vision and intent should be the responsibility of all those with a pupil-facing role, not just the inspectorate. For those who take part in PLCs, learning the range of coaching skills provides the basis for high-quality discussion and well-structured outcomes where everyone works together and can answer questions with confidence and deep understanding of their role in the process. Where individuals within the school are part of a coaching team those within PLCs and teams across the school have the benefit of a critical friend who will support them without judging or directing. Coaching creates a culture where there is no such thing as failure and where mistakes are treated as learning diamonds.

Top tips

- Put learning first in every action and decision to be made
- Define for yourself and other staff what quality means in relation to creating the highest standards in the realisation of curriculum excellence
- Ensure CPD deepens subject knowledge and builds a synergy for excellence in learning
- Allow subject and phase leaders to have autonomy in the design and implementation models for their subject or subjects
- Create time, space and resources so that teams can work together in the pursuit of a sequenced, conceptual, deep and broad curriculum from Early Years to Year 6 and beyond
- Make sure lesson observation is part of CPD and is not seen as an opportunity to find out what is going wrong
- Take great care when expecting members within teams to make changes to the way they work and perform
- Create professional learning communities with the right expertise and skills and where the goals are clearly defined by the team in line with the school vision and curriculum intent
- Create opportunities for leaders, teams, teachers and teaching assistants to learn a range of effective coaching skills including active listening and questioning skills so that there is a collective narrative that echoes what the school wants to achieve
- Instructional or incremental coaching provides a framework for supporting individuals to manage change and improve their pedagogical or planning skills

References

Aguilar, E. (2016) *The Art of Coaching Teams: Building Resilient Communities that Transform Schools*. San Francisco, CA: Jossey-Bass.

Case, S. (2005) *Leading Change in Schools: A Practical Handbook*. Stafford: Network Educational Press.

Department for Education (DfE) (2014) *National Curriculum Programmes of Study in England: Key Stage 1 & 2*. London: DfE.

Department for Education (DfE) (2016) *Standard for Teachers' Professional Development*. London: DfE.

Education Endowment Foundation (EEF) (September 2021) *Teaching and Learning Toolkit*. London: Education Endowment Foundation.

Education Endowment Foundation (EEF) (October 2021) Effective Professional Development: *Three recommendations for Designing and Selecting Effective CPD*. London: Education Endowment Foundation.

Howard, K. and Hill, C. (2020) *Symbiosis: The Curriculum and the Classroom*. Woodbridge: John Catt Educational.

Knight, J. (2007) *Instructional Coaching: A Partnership Approach to Improving Instruction.* Thousand Oaks, CA: Corwin Press.

Ofsted (2018) *Research: Assessing Intent, Implementation and Impact.* London: Ofsted.

Ofsted (2019) *Research Commentary: Inspecting Education Quality – Lesson Observation and Workbook Scrutiny.* London: Ofsted.

Scott, C. D. and Jaffe, D. T. (1988) 'Survive and Thrive in Times of Change'. *Training and Development Journal*, 42(4): 25–7.

Spielman, A. (2017) *Amanda Spielman's Speech to the Festival of Education, 2017.* [Speech transcript] Festival of Education, Wellington College, Crowthorne. 23 June 2017. Available at: https://www.gov.uk/government/speeches/amanda-spielmans-speech-at-the-festival-of-education (accessed 27 July 2022).

Stansfield, S. (2020) *Leading from the Middle, training programme.* Bridgnorth: Learning Cultures Limited.

Teaching Schools Council (2016) *Effective Primary Teaching Practice.* London: Teaching Schools Council.

van Nieuwerburgh, C. (2014) *An Introduction to Coaching Skills: A Practical Guide.* London: Sage.

Whitmore, J. (2017) *Coaching for Performance: The Principles and Practice of Coaching and Leadership, 5th edn.* London: Nicholas Brealey.

9

DRAWING TOGETHER THE STRANDS THAT DEFINE A HIGH-QUALITY CURRICULUM

A tapestry is based on a combination of threads, the weft and the warp, both threads interwoven in a way which enables the final meaningful picture to emerge, neither more important that the other, but of little value without the relationship it holds with its partner thread. Ideally, to ensure the tapestry's strength and longevity they will be held in place by a well-designed frame. (Smith, 2013: 103)

Creating the tools to deliver a high-quality curriculum

This final chapter aims to provide those who have responsibility for the unfolding of a knowledge rich and skills focused curriculum with a range of planning tools, CPD activities and coaching models that will support senior, middle and subject leaders and teachers to focus on how to begin their journey towards knowing with confidence that the curriculum on offer in their school provides an outstanding and high-quality education that ensures all pupils thrive.

Each unique school brings its own perspective and context to a framework that is designed to be flexible and that will shape learning for all sorts of different characters who pass through on their learning journey towards secondary school and their future life beyond education. The ultimate message is that the curriculum must be defined and sculpted by those who understand the local and wider context within which the school exists. It is, therefore, essential that those who hold decisions about the curriculum in their hands can communicate a coherent rationale for their choice of curriculum outcomes and share their ambition with all those with a pupil-facing role. A consistent and clear goal where the impact is well-defined at the beginning of the process strengthens the resolve of all those involved and leads to continuous professional learning and development.

Leadership and Influencing Change – Kotter's eight-stage process

Change is constant for senior leaders everywhere, never more so than in the context of a school. The curriculum is not that new now but the changing landscape of the last few years with a new Ofsted handbook, the new Early Career Framework, (last updated September 2022) changes to the EYFS curriculum have all required new thinking. The need to focus on how to make sure all pupils are moving forward with their learning due to the disruption caused by the pandemic and COVID have created new challenges for the headteacher and the senior leadership team.

We have looked in the previous chapter at the effect change can have on staff. Inertia is not uncommon when individuals feel threatened by new ideas or where reshaping of the rhythms of the way they have always worked previously has to alter. It is undoubtedly the role of the leader to manage the change process and build a culture of trust and determination that ensures new beginnings will be positive and advantageous to all those involved.

The curriculum has to be an evolving process. Reflection as to what is working well and what is having an impact on learning and achievement is essential as is a realistic focus on where there are issues or problems that require a change of thinking and a revisiting of decisions made. It is, therefore, essential to have a profound understanding of how to manage change in a positive and sensitive way. One tool that is a favourite of ours at Learning Cultures and comes with recommendations from many school leaders is Kotter's eight-stage process (Kotter, 2014). John Kotter introduced this process in his book Leading Change first published in 1995.

His eight stages, similar to climbing a ladder towards consolidating change that is sustainable. His eight stages are:

- Step 8 Institutionalise changes
- Step 7 Consolidate improvements
- Step 6 Plan and create short-term wins
- Step 5 Empower others to act on the vision
- Step 4 Communicate the vision
- Step 3 Create the vision
- Step 2 Form a powerful guiding coalition
- Step 1 Establish a sense of urgency

The first step is to establish a sense of urgency that brings all those involved together to focus on the reasons why the change is essential. The right team or guiding coalition is critical to success, knowing the strengths within the team, capitalising on the skills of each individual member and also knowing who will need training or extra resources to achieve the ultimate goal. Creating the goal or vision is essential. No one who is part of a guiding coalition can succeed if they don't know what it is they are setting out to achieve. Equally important is the need to communicate with great clarity what the vision is, what success will look like and what impact success will have on pupil achievement, staff motivation or improved behaviour and attitudes to learning. This all helps to empower others to embrace the vision.

Planning for short-term wins is an excellent tactic. Knowing certain points along the journey that can be celebrated as milestones or where a particular strategy or project has proved to work well must be celebrated and shared with others. Success is infectious and smooths the path for obstacles that may well impede progress in other places or times. However small, a short-term win is a step towards the acceptance and embracing of change.

The next two stages may take the longest time so planning how to consolidate the improvements by consistently reinforcing their importance or articulating the difference they are making will help to finally ensure they are embraced as the right way forward. Communicating how effective the named change has been and rewarding all those who have been instrumental in creating new ways of working will go some way to making sure that the change is seen as positive.

The LEARN model – a planning tool for those focusing on curriculum intent into implementation

Wherever you and your school are along the curriculum trajectory the pandemic and the effects of schools closing will have had an impact on how your future curriculum plans are decided upon. Education is an ever-changing landscape in more normal times so the disruption and challenges that have faced all those in education make the next steps essential to get right.

It is my sincere view that we have to look forward and not dwell on the past. Much of the language that has accompanied the return to school has been negative. Lost learning, catching up, gaps in learning and reduced attention spans all leave the pupil with a feeling of inadequacy that is categorically not their fault. The future is theirs and we must create a rich and varied education that will build confidence, foster motivation and lead to a love of learning.

This may be for many an ideal time to re-think the curriculum and how it is planned and delivered to focus on what is currently working well and consider where change would enhance the learning and build new possibilities into the mix which builds on good practice and creates opportunities for new and innovate ideas to flourish and grow as part of invigorating the depth and breadth of the curriculum offer.

When this current but then new curriculum was launched in 2014, we developed a model for school leaders to use as a planning and discussion tool. Wherever possible, creating a framework within which to work will reap rewards as it ensures that individuals who are part of a planning team work together within the same sphere and do not find themselves going along a different and lonely trajectory.

LEARN came out of a discussion about how to make the transition from the old curriculum model to the new one without too much disruption, too many lost resources and too much change all at once. We have changed some of the questions over time but it continues to be a welcome and well-used approach to allowing the team to think within a contained but expanding model. LEARN stands for Leave in, Explore possibilities, Amend and adapt, Reshape, New innovations.

Questions are linked to each of the phrases in order to create a robust opportunity to focus on what needs to be in place in terms of evidence of careful and consistent planning linked to collaboration and consultation.

Table 9.1 LEARN

L.E.A.R.N.	Questions to challenge and consider
Leave in	• What currently works well as part of the observation process that you will leave in? • How long for? • What elements of your current curriculum have a positive impact on learning and achievement for teachers and pupils? • How can we make the best use of what we have in place to inform change and challenge?
Explore possibilities	• What are our strengths as a school? • How can we build on our strengths and implement changes that will make a difference? • What CPD needs will help to fill gaps in our knowledge and understanding about the curriculum? • How would change impact on school and pupil continuous improvement? • Who can we identify as those who can lead the process of change?
Amend and adapt	• What can we identify that needs amending or adapting? • How can we share ideas and resources so that we can adapt what we know has worked in the past? • What is available that we can use to enhance our current systems without too much work? • How can we influence change without causing anxiety?
Replace	• What do we know needs to be replaced? • How will we communicate the need to make change happen? • How will we create the right culture where individuals feel comfortable with change? • How will we manage those who are uncomfortable with proposed changes?
New innovations	• What could we introduce that is completely new and different? • What are the training and development implications? • How will we monitor success and the impact on learning?

So, Table 9.1 shows some of the questions for a team to work with, this model can be adapted to all sorts of situations where change is required.

This model allows individuals to focus on what is working well and encourages the consolidation of good practice and a status quo as well as embracing the need to look for new ideas that can either replace older practices or amend them for a new and refreshing look at things.

The curriculum as a tapestry of learning – weaving all the pieces together

For those who are implementing the curriculum the focus must be on outcomes and how through careful planning and a deep understanding of the depth of knowledge within a particular subject pupils will gain deep insights and learn well.

Curriculum, subject and phase leaders and teachers must also be clear as to the core skills of literacy and numeracy that pupils will need in order to access the knowledge. These skills are taught discretely in maths and English and are integral to learning in every other subject. It is, however, not just to numeracy and literacy that we must pay attention – it is also to the wider metacognitive skills that bind learning and deepen understanding as well as equipping pupils with valuable skills for life.

Ofsted's research in 2019, referred to in Chapter 3, offers an opportunity to focus on what inspectors want to see from observing learning in the classroom. The 18 indicators that were the result of that piece of research are linked to what the teacher is doing. They are valuable in providing all teachers and those who observe them with a tool to support their endeavours to plan and implement the curriculum that will marry with the Ofsted handbook quality of education judgement (Ofsted, 2022). Observing the teacher is important but so is looking in detail at what outcomes we would want to see by observing the pupils' response to the different pedagogy and classroom management seen in the classroom. Table 9.2 shows a list of some of the outcomes one would hope to find from a deep dive into how pupils respond to their teacher. As part of a CPD activity these phrases can be made into cards that early career, recently qualified and experienced teachers can use to share where they see these pupil outcomes link to the teacher observation indicators.

Focusing on the learning as well as the teaching ensures a clear focus on what is the most important element in the process of collaborative learning, which is the achievement and well-being of the pupil.

A vision and rationale for curriculum design

Table 9.3 is a blueprint that subject leaders can use as part of their planning and to create opportunities to work closely with their subject teams in a spirit of creating a curriculum plan that links together all of the elements that are essential in building a coherent and high-quality curriculum map across the year groups and key stages.

The opportunity for teachers to work together within their subject teams with some kind of framework will help to create the evidence that there is a collaborative approach to curriculum implementation and ensure that whoever takes a deep dive into the planning, the teaching and the assessment will find a united voice and a commitment to excellence. Create a proforma with the questions so that individuals in their teams can work together and record their discussions and plans. Teams need to be looking specifically at the component parts of the curriculum that need to be included, the priorities for change and the goals for impact.

Table 9.2 A focus on observing the pupil in the classroom linked to what is deemed high-quality teaching and learning

Pupils can link their learning to what they already know	Teachers check that pupils are deepening their knowledge and becoming increasingly competent in a range of skills
Pupils can make connections with other subjects or cross curricular learning	Pupils are given access to rich texts and increasingly complex tasks that will broaden their understanding
All pupils have access to the same content and knowledge	Progression opportunities are clearly defined
Pupils have the confidence to accept challenge and intervention	Pupils have retained the knowledge from previous learning and know how to use that learning to inform new learning
Intervention is planned so that all pupils can access the curriculum	Pupils are able to use their previous understanding as a springboard for deeper learning
Gaps in learning and in skills development are understood and actions taken to support pupils	There is clarity as to what is being assessed in relation to knowledge and skills
Pupils are engaged throughout the lesson	Pupils know what is expected of them in the work they produce
There are opportunities for all pupils to deepen their learning using a wide range of pedagogies	Pupils are encouraged to reflect on their own learning journey
Pupils are listened to and respond to deep and rich questioning so that they can discuss how they are learning	Where pupils are stuck they can respond to challenge
Pupils can access the presentations teachers use and have sufficient challenge within them	Pupils demonstrate that they can understand meaning in the work that is given to them
Resources used in lessons are highly interactive and help deepen pupils' knowledge and understanding	Pupils are challenged to find solutions and solve problems for themselves
Feedback to pupils is seen as the way to improve the quality of work or output and never seen as a criticism of what is not right	Pupils are given the opportunity to explain their understanding and have deep clarity as to the way they learn
Pupils have high self-esteem and are contributors to their own learning and to others' learning	There are clear and consistent expectations that all pupils adhere to. They know the boundaries and what will happen if they transcend those boundaries
Pupils are engaged, interested and challenged to achieve more. The culture in the classroom negates low-level disruption	Each pupil is working with subject matter that will challenge them and extend their capacity
Pupils know that challenge is part of learning	Each pupil knows that their teacher supports them in their quest for deeper learning

Table 9.3 Building a consensus of how to turn intent into implementation

What content will be taught across all subjects?	How is the learning sequenced?	How will learning be assessed?	What is the ambition for all pupils?	What skills and concepts will be woven through the learning?
Schema Programmes of study Syllabus Specification Depth of Knowledge Parity for all Identifying which topics Weaving in SMSC/PSHE	Building on prior learning Creating a continuum of learning Working towards defined end points Defining where learning overlaps Making connections Identifying key concepts Building at points of transition	Summative assessment Formative assessment Mixed ability Streaming/ setting Assessing knowledge, skills and thinking Attitudes and beliefs Connections across all learning Qualitative and quantitative data	Achieve their full potential Accept challenge Be confident and motivated to learn Are equipped for the next stage of learning Understand their world and their place in it Be enquiring, innovative and collaborative	Reading is seen as a priority at every stage Mathematical fluency and confidence in numeracy Ability to use higher levels of response Developing a wide range of thinking skills Effective communication skills Ability to share ideas and debate

Creating the unconsciously competent learner – skills at the heart of deep learning

The primary years are an essential time for all pupils to gain a range of skills that will allow them to access and use knowledge for the rest of their education and beyond for life and work. The aim for all those involved in deciding what to teach and how to teach it must be to ensure that by the time pupils reach the end of Year 6 they have become competent in their ability to read, write, speak and listen with confidence and clarity. Equally, they should have mastered the relevant age-related standards in maths. Just as important is their proficiency in the use of both literacy and numeracy skills where they are integral to learning in science and all of the other foundation subjects. There is a tacit acknowledgement that knowledge is important. However, without the relevant skills no pupil will be able to access that knowledge and build a bank of learning that will last them a lifetime.

Developing the skills for learning requires practice, opportunities to recall prior learning and the self-confidence to be resilient in the face of failure. We like the model of growing competence (Broadwell, 1969) that starts with:

- **The state of unconscious incompetence** – the learner has never encountered the need to use this skill before and is therefore unaware that they can't do it

- **The state of conscious incompetence** – the learner tries out the new skill and is now conscious of their incompetence
- **The state of conscious competence** – with practice, reinforcement, reward and support the learner is learning the skill and is beginning to feel confident with their progress
- **The state of unconscious competence** – the learner has mastered the skill and can use it without even realising that they are using the skill that gave them some trouble in the past

One can easily draw an analogy to learning to drive that anyone who has been through that process, and that is most of us, can relate to the model. There is a fifth competence that is sometimes added here which is reflective competence – once we have acquired and mastered the skill how can we continue to improve and grow.

Applying this same model to creating opportunities for pupils to use their growing repertoire of skills will help them to become unconsciously competent in their use. Planning the curriculum should absolutely include the deliberate and regular reinforcement of how pupil's use their literacy, numeracy and metacognitive skills in as many contexts as possible. The model suggests that reinforcement, reward and regular feedback have a greater effect on moving the pupil forward than deliberate support and training or teaching.

Monitoring skills development and ensuring data is available so that teachers know which pupils have not mastered certain of the skills they need for learning is critical. It is so easy for a pupil to remain forever at the stage of conscious incompetence if they learn that they 'can't do it'. Reinforcing this limiting belief is easy when pupils fall off the radar.

It is a good idea to break down the skills that all teachers should be dovetailing into their plans. Below is a list of the skills that are essential and an integral part of the curriculum programmes of study. Table 9.4 illuminates the essential skills set out in the programmes of study for English and maths. Providing opportunities for teachers to share their practice in how they teach these skills in English or maths and across the foundation subjects is useful CPD.

Table 9.4 Literacy and numeracy applies across the whole curriculum and not just in English and maths

English	English cont.....	Maths
Reading for research	Creative writing	Calculations
Reading for information	Answering questions	Estimating and checking problems
Reading non-fiction	Discussion	Reasoning and problem solving
Reading fiction	Presentation	Measuring
Poetry	Listening	Geometry
Writing essays	The language of assessment	Data handling
Comprehension	Writing for pleasure	Use of graphs, charts and tables

For each of the above, perhaps with the exception of reading fiction, poetry and creative writing, all of the other areas for development are not exclusive to English or maths. Even fiction, poetry and creative writing can have their place in subjects like history, MFL or art and music, thus spreading the imagination to build innovative learning opportunities that allow pupils to become consciously and unconsciously competent abound.

Planning tools that weave together sequential knowledge and skills

Creating a scheme of work that creates the tapestry that depicts a knowledge-rich, sequenced conceptual map of learning is not easy. There is a lot to put in there. The topic or subject objectives need to come first. These should be:

- Specific to the topic content and relate to the subject purpose of study, aims and subject content
- Linked to skills that pupils will use to access and process the subject content
- Focus on building prior knowledge and understanding
- Focus on outcomes for pupils learning collectively but with an eye on differentiation throughout the topic

The proforma that teachers should use must be uniform across all subjects and shared so that teachers delivering the topic to their year group, phase or key stage all work together to create a seamless and progressive plan that links back to the school's vision and intent. Table 9.5 gives examples of what some headings might be.

The wider skills include the metacognitive or thinking skills that undoubtedly create opportunities for pupils to deepen their learning and become problem-solvers, risk-takers and powerful communicators. Enquiry, note-taking, debate, reflection, peer-to-peer and group interaction, analysis, experimentation, all come under this category.

To make the best use of a set of parameters such as those set out above, a sheet of A3 paper is better than A4. The headings need to be on every page otherwise the content becomes difficult to follow and it is wise to retain it electronically with permission

Table 9.5 Designing a scheme of work that embraces all the different elements of a high-quality curriculum offer

Sequence of learning within the topic to deepen knowledge	What do pupils already know in order to build on their knowledge and understanding?	What *literacy skills* will be developed/further developed in order that pupils can demonstrate deep knowledge, understanding and progression?	What *numeracy skills* will be developed/further developed in order that pupils can demonstrate deep knowledge, understanding and progression?	What *other wider skills* will support the learning linked to deepening knowledge, fostering progression and demonstrating mastery?

restrictions so that the collective team involved in the making of the document can make changes. Other teams can have read-only access whereby they can liaise and make suggestions that can be altered by the designated team.

Sequencing the knowledge – creating a taxonomy for progression

The sequencing of the learning over time is essential in creating the evidence that the curriculum does indeed have depth and breadth and ensures that pupils progress well over their time in the primary school.

The programmes of study for maths, English and science are broken down into age-related standards that use progressive verbs to create a sequence of learning over time. These relate to Bloom's taxonomy or to any model of progression linked to a framework for deepening learning over time. So if we take the science curriculum, (Table 9.6 taken from the science programme of study at Key Stage 1 & 2 DfE, 2014) the deepening of learning is clearly laid out. I have chosen just a couple of the strands that make up a sequence from EYFS to Year 6.

The foundation subjects do not have the same chronological detail attached to their programmes of study but there is a wealth of detail included in the narrative that explains the purpose of study and the aims for each different subject. For instance, in history similar verbs state the expected outcomes for pupils. For this and other foundation subjects it is the subject leader and teachers who have to look at the statutory requirements and create for themselves the sequence of learning that pupils follow in order to learn and deepen their knowledge over time.

In history, for example, the purpose of study is to ensure pupils have a coherent knowledge and understanding of the past, while the teaching should inspire pupils' curiosity to know more about the past, ask perceptive questions and think critically. They should be able to weigh evidence, sift arguments, develop perspective and make judgements. The teaching should help pupils to understand the process of change, the diversity of societies and the relationships between different groups.

The aims reveal more about what teachers need to do to shape a sequential curriculum. Pupils should know and understand as well as gain and deploy knowledge and understand historical concepts such as continuity and change. They should be able to make connections and explain similarities and differences and the significance of events as well as draw contrasts and analyse trends. They should be able to frame historical questions, create their own narratives and gain historical perspective.

Each foundation subject has a similar format and all shine a spotlight on the need to create opportunities for pupils to deepen their knowledge and understanding through challenging and increasingly complex tasks and learning activities over time.

Table 9.6 The verbs that create a progressive and sequential science curriculum from Early Years to Year 6

EYFS	Year 1	Year 2	Year 3	Year 4	Year 5	Year 6
Children know about **similarities and differences** in relation to living things	**Identify** and name a variety of common wild and garden plants	**Explore and compare** the difference between things living and dead	**Identify functions** of different parts of flowering plants, roots etc	**Recognise** that living things can be grouped in a variety of ways	**Describe the differences** in the **life cycle** of a mammal, an amphibian, an insect and a bird	**Describe** how living things are **classified** into broad groups to common observable characteristics
Children **make observations** of animals and plants	**Identify and name** a variety of common animals. **Describe and compare structures** of a variety of common animals	**Identify how** seeds and bulbs grow. **Find out and describe how** plants need water, light and temperature to grow	**Investigate** the way in which water is transplanted within plants. **Compare and group** together different kinds of rocks	**Describe** the simple functions of the basic parts of the digestive systems in humans	**Explain** that unsupported objects fall towards the earth **because** of the force of gravity	**Recognise** that light appears to travel in straight lines **Use the idea** that light travels in straight lines to **explain** that objects are seen because they reflect light into the eye

Some of the questions that must form a part of teacher development and a shared narrative must include (I have used the history programme of study here but the questions will be similar for all foundation subjects):

- What should pupils know and understand by the end of Year 6?
- How do teachers inspire curiosity in their subject?
- How do subject leaders and teachers create the right pedagogy so that pupils learn to ask perceptive questions and think critically?
- What are the skills pupils need to weigh evidence, sift arguments, develop perspective and make judgements?
- What kinds of activities and teaching sequences will help pupils to make connections and explain similarities and differences
- How can we teach pupils to draw contrasts, analyse trends or data and use evidence to draw their own narrative or verbal responses?

Conceptual understanding – creating connections to strengthen learning

Concepts abound within subjects and can transcend subject boundaries, making it difficult sometimes for pupils to fully understand how to make connections and use vocabulary that is relevant in more than one subject. Perspectives in history are not the same as perspective in art but the word has the same meaning in relation to seeing things differently from different angles. Light is a concept but it is dealt with very differently in science and in art. Resistance is repelling something but in history it also has different meanings such as resistance to war or in science the properties of different rocks in their ability to resist being eroded away too quickly.

Within each subject it is a good idea to explore the concepts that are evident within the subject and then to create an opportunity for teachers from different subjects to work together to see where concepts transcend the subject divides and have similar or different meanings or contexts. Creating a shared understanding of the importance of conceptual learning for teachers must reap huge benefits for ensuring pupils have a similar exposure and begin to develop a vocabulary that deepens their ability to remember and to ensure the learning is remembered over time.

Formative assessment – a critical element of implementation

A critical element of planning the primary curriculum is defining the impact the content in relation to skills, knowledge, sequencing and conceptual understanding will have on pupils' achievement and attainment at the end of Year 6. It is, therefore,

Table 9.7 Ideas for a set of cards to support teachers to talk about formative assessment

Sharing learning outcomes with pupils	Using annotated examples of different levels of response	Feed forward, what next? What else? How?
Sharing success criteria with pupils	Encouraging peer to peer discussions about learning	Creating opportunities for collaborative group work
Making key learning words visible	Focusing on comprehension and deeper understanding through reading	Creating opportunities for reciprocal teaching
Creating a bank of subject specific vocabulary	Using higher order questioning	Allowing peer to peer assessment of their work
Using planning and writing frames	Allowing wait-time or silence to allow the pupil to organise their responses	Comment only marking Modelling the answer for pupils to replicate

essential that the planning process includes a deep understanding of what will be assessed along the learning journey from EYFS and then within and at the end of each year to Year 6. Formative assessment is a pedagogy and should be seen as part of classroom management in every lesson. How are learners progressing? What are their gaps in learning? What are common misconceptions that need correcting? How do we make sure pupils are challenged and stretched to achieve and exceed their potential?

Table 9.7 is a list of phrases that can be turned into cards that will provide an opportunity for subject leads and teachers to share their strategies for formative assessment and discuss what works and what can be improved upon.

Ten approaches to create a consistent whole-school formative assessment strategy

Here are some ideas that may help to build a consensus as to how learning is assessed consistently across all subjects.

- Assessment should be constructive and positive and take account of the emotional impact it can have on learner motivation
- Assessment should be motivating and encourage the learner to want to learn more
- There should be a consistent whole-school approach that ensures assessment is linked to clearly defined outcomes and how they should be assessed
- Assessment should be about how learners can improve and give the learner very clear direction about what they do well (their strengths) and sensitively focus on their 'weaknesses' (gaps) in their learning
- Assessment should include opportunities for reflection where the learner assesses their own learning as part of a process of self-assessment
- Assessing learning is a fundamental skill and all teachers should have the ability to articulate what this means
- Assessment should be an integral pedagogy that is central to a learning classroom
- Learning is complex and the greater the opportunity to ensure learners are made aware of the skills they are using to access and retain knowledge the deeper will be their understanding

- Assessment is an essential element of planning and delivery of the curriculum
- Assessment should take account of different starting points, the range of abilities and the need for stretch and challenge for some or maybe all learners

Using the above ten approaches provides opportunities for those who are planning the assessment policy and action plan to focus on the following:

- Assessment as part of curriculum planning and implementation
- Collaboration and partnership working for subject leaders and teachers
- Teaching and learning strategies including involving pupils in their own self-assessment
- CPD needs for all those involved in the process of assessment
- Parity for learners with special educational needs and disabilities

Summative assessment has its place and low-stakes testing, quizzes and tests can be a good way to assess all pupils in a consistent way but there is no substitute for the ongoing formative assessment that has a positive impact on learning over time.

This mnemonic can be something for senior leaders to use as a starting point for discussing a plan for making sure their assessment strategies provide the right evidence for any form of 'deep dive'.

Take time to define the strategy

Interweave assessment into the planned curriculum

Communicate and collaborate to ensure clarity of purpose

Know the coaching and assessment skills that impact on learning and progression

Building a consensus and working together to deliver impact

Using the contents of this book to reflect on how the curriculum is planned and delivered provides an opportunity to assess what is currently working well and what could strengthen decisions about the depth and breadth of what is taught and the clarity of purpose to ensure that pupils are motivated and enthusiastic about wanting to learn, to solve their own problems and take risks with their learning.

The flexibility, certainly in the foundation subjects, to develop curriculum content that ignites the curiosity for pupils to find out more about their own local context and link it to discovering new and exciting vistas of learning that are out there in the wider context is profound. The core, although more prescriptive in terms of age-related standards, still provides great scope for expanding the minds of pupils who can then apply their learning in all sorts of new contexts.

Table 9.8 outlines a set of priorities that are phrases that can be recreated as a set of cards for teams to use to work out their priorities in relation to their own setting, reflect on what they currently do well, and begin to put together a plan to enhance learning,

Table 9.8 Creating a card sort tool for a deep dive into curriculum intent and implementation

There is breadth across a full range of subjects	Differentiation matches learning to learner attainment	Skills are developed in relation to accessing learning, deepening learning and ensuring progression
There is a balance of time, subject content and skills development	Progression extends learning, knowledge, skills and understanding	Deepening understanding enables pupils to construct meaning
Content is relevant to learners' needs and experience	Knowledge is linked to learning in and across subject divides	We promote positive attitudes to learning and attitudes about learning
There is coherence so that the content interrelates	Conceptual learning is applied in a variety of contexts across the curriculum	Subject vocabulary is comprehended and allows learners to access knowledge and make connections across all their learning
There is interweaving of discrete subjects	Learning is re-enforced so that the knowledge is retained in the long term memory	Attention is paid to prior learning especially at times of transition
Learning is sequenced so that learners build on their learning over time	Pupils are challenged to achieve more	Effort is rewarded
Assessment is designed as part of curriculum planning to ensure learners achieve the stated outcomes		

Designed by the curriculum team at Learning Cultures to evoke discussion about curriculum intent and implementation.

progression and achievement over time. Consensus and discussion ripple out and from initial senior leader collaboration there is much more likelihood that the curriculum intent translates into a clearly defined pathway for all those who manage and teach to follow.

Start by asking the question, which of the following phrases can we confidently agree with and which ones need some work?

In this final chapter I have endeavoured to provide some tools and ideas to support senior, subject and team leaders to work together with teachers to create a knowledge-rich and skills-focused curriculum that is engaging, creative and much more than just a set of external standards to be achieved. Bringing the curriculum alive with exciting pedagogy and illuminating resources that inspire learning and a desire to find out more is surely the essential rationale. Where leaders, teachers, their pupils and the wider community know how they are contributing to building successful futures for their school a deep dive can be awe-inspiring.

Conclusion

Current policy and the message from the inspectorate and many other commentators is that the curriculum is the 'substance' that creates the opportunities for deep learning. Defining what will be taught and how it will be taught should ensure all pupils are successfully accessing the curriculum and will have the knowledge and skills that will create the springboard for the next stage of their education.

Another way of looking at the importance of the curriculum is to look beyond the substance and focus on the quality of outcome that is the ultimate measure of success for a school in relation to their choices with regard to what will be taught and when. Quality is a relative term. It is up to the senior leadership team and other curriculum leaders to define the level of quality they expect from all of those with responsibility for delivering the curriculum intent. They need to have a very clear definition of their version of quality and be able to translate it into purposeful activity that leads to excellence and continuous improvement for all.

It has been my aim throughout the writing of this book to provide all those who have a responsibility in some way for providing high-quality learning outcomes for their pupils to have practical as well as informed strategies that will create a shared commitment to high-quality, innovative and exciting learning opportunities for all pupils, whatever their starting point, background or disadvantages. Primary years education including the early years are so important in creating the right springboard for ongoing and future learning and are so rewarding when we see pupils flourish and grow. It is a privilege to share my own learning journey through the primary curriculum and to be a part of a tomorrow that will build new futures for all of us who have a passion for education.

Top tips

- The curriculum must be defined and shaped by those who understand the local and wider context within which the school exists
- Be clear as to the rationale for the choices regarding curriculum content, outcomes and ambition for pupils and communicate it widely
- Understand the impact change has on individual staff members
- Manage change through the building of a culture of trust and a determination to ensure change is positive and ultimately beneficial
- Look forward and use past events to see how what has happened can be positive in strengthening future plans and developments
- Always focus on what is working well, before considering what needs to change
- Be clear as to the core skills of literacy and numeracy pupils must have to access knowledge. Marry these with the metacognitive or learning to learn skills
- Teams need to work together on the curriculum priorities for change and goals for impact
- Create opportunities for pupils to make connections across all their learning
- Break down the skills included in the English and maths programmes of study and use them with the foundation subjects to see how integral all the skills are to learning elsewhere
- Focus on the purpose of study and the aims at the beginning of each of the programmes of study – they create a good starting point for planning
- Be imaginative, encourage innovation and create the inspired pupil

References

Broadwell, M. M. (1969) *'The Four Stages of Competence'*. included in an article in the National School. Improvement Network, Institute of Education. Research Matters publication (2022). Original source: Broadwell, M. M. (1969) 'Teaching for Learning (XVI.)', The Gospel Guardian, Vol. 20, No 41, pp. 1–3

Department for Education (DfE) (2014) *National Curriculum Programmes of Study in England: Key Stage 1 & 2*. London: DfE.

Department for Education (DfE) (2021) *Statutory Framework for the Early Years Foundation Stage*. London: DfE.

Department for Education (DfE) (2022) *Early Career Framework*. London: DfE.

Kotter, J. P. (2012) *Leading Change*. Boston, MA: Harvard Business Review Press.

Kotter, J. P. (2014) *Accelerate*. Boston, MA: Harvard Business Review Press.

Ofsted (2019) *Research Commentary: Inspecting Education Quality – Lesson Observation and Workbook Scrutiny*. London: Ofsted.

Ofsted (2022) *School Inspection Handbook*. London: Ofsted.

Smith, D. (2013) 'A Tapestry Curriculum'. In Blatchford, R. (ed.) *Taking Forward the Primary Curriculum: Applying the 2014 National Curriculum for KS1 and KS2*. Woodbridge: John Catt Educational.

INDEX

Note: Page references with *f* denote figures and with *t* tables.